Testify

Testify

K.R. Bowman

iUniverse, Inc.
New York   Bloomington

Testify
How I got to here from there

Unless otherwise indicated, Scripture quotations are from the Holy Bible, New International Version Copyright 1973, 1978, 1984 by International Bible Society. Used by permission of Zondervan. All rights reserved.

Scripture quotations marked (KJV) are taken from the King James Version of the Holy Bible.

iUniverse books may be ordered through booksellers or by contacting:

iUniverse
1663 Liberty Drive
Bloomington, IN 47403
www.iuniverse.com
1-800-Authors (1-800-288-4677)

ISBN: 978-1-4401-2854-7 (sc)
ISBN: 978-1-4401-2855-4 (ebook)

Printed in the United States of America

iUniverse rev. date: 03/09/2009

In loving memory of my mother
Kathleen Davis
and my mother-in-law
Beva Frye
who are with Jesus

To Donna Searle, Mom, thanks for all the time you have invested in me and the production of my autobiography.

Introduction

I was born on October 27, 1958, to Mr. and Mrs. Van Ray Bowman, in Gulfport, Mississippi. I had a sister Brenda who was 2 1/2 years older. By the time I was two, my parents had separated and gotten a divorce. At the young age of two I remember my father kneeling down, telling my sister and me that he would not be living with us any more, but that he would be seeing us whenever he could. My mother married another man who became my stepdad.

At three years of age I remember my sister and I playing on the beach, on the Gulf coast across the road from where we lived. Also we lived next door to an American Indian family with a young boy my age. We would play cowboys and indians. He would want to play the part of the cowboy and I would play the part of the indian.

At four years of age we moved to northern Mississippi to Carthage, where my mother was born and raised. We lived at an old farm house that was in my mother's family. I remember taking baths in number three wash tubs that were filled with water in the mornings so the sun could warm the water by evening. I remember we had a little black dog that would wait for me to walk by him in the yard. As I would go past him he would run up to me from behind and grab a hold of my underwear and pull them down. It's funny now as I think back on it, but it wasn't to me as a four year old youngster.

One night coming home after we had been in town doing laundry, we noticed the night sky lighted up. As we got closer to our house, the road was lined up on both sides with automobiles. Then as we drove up to where our house was, there were fire trucks trying to contain the fire. Our house was totally engulfed in flames. I remember sitting there watching the flames. To the left of the house was a big tree I would play under. Underneath the tree was my pedal tractor crumbling to a pile of rubbish from the intense heat coming from the fire. At four years of age I was not thinking about where we might have to live now or where we might even have to sleep, or was I thinking that everything we had in the world except two loads of clothes was lost in that fire. All I could think about was my pedal tractor I would never ride or play with again.

We moved from there to a small town in the middle of the state, Magee. I remember in elementary school I took a goldfish out of the fish bowl to play with before lunch break. When the school bell rang I laid the fish on the table and went to eat. When we returned the fish had dried out and had died. My teacher was not very sympathetic with me. She called my mother, who had to go to the school and pay for the fish. How much could a goldfish cost in 1964?

From the time my biological parents separated until I was eleven years of age, my sister and I would spend one weekend a month and six weeks in the summer with my father and my stepmom. I remember as a young boy getting dressed up on Sunday mornings and going to church with them when we stayed at their house. They attended a Presbyterian Church in Carthage, Mississippi, where they lived. They both had a part in seeing that I was brought up in a loving Christian home. When I was at home with my mother and stepdad I do not recall going to church early on in my life like I did when I visited my father. But at the age of nine I do remember my mother, my stepdad, my brothers, my sisters and myself all going to church at First Baptist Church in Magee, Mississippi. And so my testimony begins. 1 Peter 3:15 says, "But in your hearts set apart Christ as Lord. Always be prepared to give an answer to everyone who asks you to give the reason for the hope that you have. But do this with gentleness and respect."

Chapter One

It began like any other Sunday morning when I was nine years old. I was awakened by my stepdad and went through the kitchen where my mother was busy fixing breakfast. She made the best homemade biscuits along with eggs, grits, and bacon or sausage. After eating we were all busy getting ready for church. There were eight of us to get ready. My stepdad, mother, three sisters, two brothers and myself. We got the typical lecture on the way to the First Baptist Church, Behave yourselves, no yelling, no running, listen to your Sunday school teachers.

After Sunday school was over and before the church service had started I was running up and down the stairs that went from the Sunday school classes to the sanctuary. All of a sudden in the stairway was my stepdad who did not have a nice face on. He was not pleased with me at all. On the way up to the sanctuary for the church service he said these famous words: "When we get home you are going to get it."

We went inside and all I could think about was the whipping I would be getting later. But sometime during the message the pastor was giving God spoke to my heart. In the gospel of John 6:44, Jesus said, "No one can come to me unless the Father who sent me draws him." When the invitation came I got up and went forward. I looked beside me and my stepdad and my oldest sister were standing there with me. We all three asked Jesus into our hearts. In John 3:3, Jesus declared, "I tell you the truth, no one can see the kingdom of God unless he is born again."

When we got home I remember my stepdad telling me in light of what we had done in church he was not going to punish me this time, but I needed to realize how important it was to behave at church from now on. A week later we were all three baptized, by immersion, in the name of the Father, the Son, and the Holy Spirit. We went to church every week and my sister and I joined the children's choir and went to children's group ministry weekly.

I remember how much I enjoyed singing even at such a young age. Psalm 100:1-2 (KJV) *Make a joyful noise unto the Lord, all ye lands. Serve the Lord with gladness: come before his presence with singing.* I can only imagine what a joy it must bring to our Father in heaven to hear little children singing about him.

When I was thirteen years old our yard had become a meeting place for many kids. Not only did we have our friends over to play, but our yard was the place to be. You see, we lived in town but we had 2 1/2 city lots, so our yard was one of the biggest in our neighborhood. So when a bunch of kids wanted to play baseball, kickball or football they would show up at our house.

I remember gathering the kids around and telling them Bible stories I had learned at church or I would read to them from the Bible before we would play. My yard my rules; if you wanted to play you had to listen to me first then we would play. And I don't remember getting any arguments about it either. How happy it made me feel to share Jesus the only way I knew how at that time of my life. In Mark 10:14, "Jesus said, 'Let the little children come to me, and do not hinder them, for the kingdom of God belongs to such as these."

I think back to that time in my life and wonder why did I do that? What possible explanation could I think of for doing that? All I can come up with is my heart must have just been opened enough, and my ears in tune to the Lord enough for him to use me. God is not looking to use perfect people, but people who are obedient and willing to listen to him.

There is no age limit for people God will use if we are willing. God can and will use you for his service. In 2 Kings 11:21, "Joash was seven years old when he began to reign." Joash became a king at the age of seven. It goes on to say that he reigned for forty years. The high priest Jehoiada instructed him. And Joash did what was right in the eyes of the Lord. Why? Because he was given godly instruction by his high priest and he did it.

In Joshua chapter 14 we read about Caleb. He was eighty-five years old when he went into the land that the Lord had promised to give him through Moses. And Caleb went to battle and took the land for his inheritance at eighty-five years of age.

By the age of fifteen my family and I were going to a smaller Baptist church. I was singing in the adult choir along with my older sister and my mother. Our pastor at that time was also our song leader for the choir and the church. I was in the front row of the choir one Sunday when the pastor grabbed me by the arm and pulled me out. He took my place in the front row and just stood there singing and grinning. After that choir song was over he asked me to lead the rest of the church in the next hymn. After the church service the pastor asked me to lead the singing at church from then on. I told him I didn't know how to read music. He said, "I don't care about that, you know all the songs and you have a great set of lungs." So I agreed to give it a try and led the singing for the next few months. I was so nervous standing in front of the congregation, but I just stood firm and led them singing each week. I prayed that God would help me and give me the strength to do this small job that the pastor had entrusted me with. And even though I didn't like being up in front of everyone and felt unqualified I did what I could for the Lord.

In Judges 6:12, an angel of the Lord appeared to Gideon while he was threshing wheat and said to him, "The Lord is with you, mighty warrior." Now as the story progresses in chapter 7, Gideon raises up a large army of thirty-two thousand to fight against the Midianites who had been oppressing the Israelites. But so they would not boast that they won the battle themselves, the Lord told Gideon to send home all that were trembling with fear. Twenty-two thousand men left, while ten thousand men remained, but the Lord said there were still too many. So he gave them another test. They went to the river and some drank water from kneeling down but three hundred of them drank by lapping from their hands. And in verse 7 it says, "With the three hundred men that lapped I will save you and give the Midianites into your hands." Gideon and his men won that battle with the help of the Lord. Gideon was just a farmer but the Lord turned him into a mighty warrior by calling him out and Gideon being willing and obedient.

At the age of eighteen is when I began to have my first contemplation of suicide in my life. I'm not sure why all of a sudden it came about but it did. A lot of different things that had happened in my life just seemed to have come to surface at that time. I did not know how to deal with it and I did not ask for help. I used to keep a journal at that time of my life and I looked at it the other day. From my journal it seemed like everything in my world was on my back. Other than just finishing high school and working full time at a grocery store cutting meat, my life seemed to be a mess. My stepdad didn't approve of my friends, my music, or my independence. He was very strict with my older sister and me, but with the younger kids which were my mother's and his together he wasn't. At that time in my life I was old enough to realize also some things that had been going on in our house since I was a young boy that just were not right. And it affected me mentally and so that affected me spiritually as well.

For some reason we weren't going to church that much anymore. Something happened that my stepdad didn't like so we had stopped going as a family. But some of us were going every now and then. The last entry in my journal I wrote, *the only reason I had not taken my own life was I did not want to spend eternity in hell.* Thank God I knew there was a heaven and a hell, because if not, I believe I would have ended it right then. I was focusing at that time on everything bad or negative that had happened in my life. My mindset had become like the Israelites wandering around in the desert. They kept focusing on everything negative, not what God had done well for them. I had taken my mind off of what Jesus had done for me and was focusing on negative thoughts, selfish thoughts, self-pitying thoughts.

I wrote in my journal *my whole family is ill all the time, my work gets me upset, I have talked to God about it and have rejected him.* I wrote: *I go to bed and do not even pray.* I had let my spiritual guard down by not attending church regularly, by not reading and meditating on the word every day, by not praying to my heavenly Father everyday for guidance. 2 Timothy 1:7 (KJV) *For God hath not given us the spirit of fear; but of power, and of love; and of sound mind.*

My last entry into my journal was on September 17, 1977, so something happened and I left the following day. With nothing

K. R. Bowman

but the clothes on my back I moved in with my best friend Terry and another guy from work. Friends and other people I didn't even know gave me clothes. I had to buy transportation because the truck I was paying for and using at home was taken away from me because it was in my mother's name. My stepdad thought that would keep me from moving out but it didn't. I moved in with my pal Terry. For the last five years we had spent a lot of time together camping, fishing, working, attending school, and skipping school, being good ole boys and also getting into some minor trouble together. I bought a motorcycle at that time because that's all I could afford.

The next few weeks life was better and I was happier. I was hanging out with my best friend and roommate that was more like a brother to me than a friend. When we were not working, on Saturday night we would go to the disco clubs, drink and dance, if you called what we did dancing.

On October 26, 1977, the day before my ninetieth birthday, Terry borrowed my motorcycle and I took his truck. He was going on a ride to visit his dad out in the country and said he would be back in about an hour or two at the latest. Two hours went by. No Terry, so I went looking for him. I rode around town, no sight of him. Finally I rode out to his dad's house and he told me, he hadn't seen Terry.

I'm starting to get worried now. I headed back to town and stopped at a convenience store. I was picking something off of one of the shelves when all of a sudden someone came in and told the clerk behind the counter that Terry was dead. I ran up to him and asked, "What did you say?" And he confirmed what I did not want to hear. Terry, my best friend, had not made it through a curve in the road and plowed through a barbed wire fence. I was devastated. Not only had my best friend been killed, but he was riding my motorcycle when he died. Now I not only had to deal with the loss of my pal, my roommate, my Christian brother, for he had given his life to Jesus earlier also. I had to deal with the fact that he died while riding my motorcycle. And if that wasn't enough, the evening of his viewing at the funeral home, I was standing at the casket with tears running down my face. My stepdad walked up, looked down at Terry, leaned over towards me, and whispered, "If you boys had not have left your homes where you belong he would still be here." That was not what I needed to hear. I needed to be comforted. I needed for him to tell me it was not my fault that Terry had died.

After the funeral I did nothing but go to work and visit Terry's gravesite. Day or night, it didn't matter. I would visit the gravesite in the middle of the night if I could not sleep. I would just sit there and talk to the grave. I knew he wasn't there. I knew he was in heaven, but I was still drawn to that gravesite.

I began having recurring dreams about Terry. He would always be standing at a distance waving at me and saying, "I miss you. Why don't you come and be with me here and we can be together?" then turn and run away. I would wake up from the dream and be very upset and begin to cry. The suicide demon I was dealing with was not only in my thoughts like before. Now it was in my dreams.

When I finally realized those dreams were trying to get me to kill myself, I knew I could not deal with this myself. In Hebrews13:5, "God has said, Never will I leave you; never will I forsake you." God is always waiting to hear from his children. I cried out to God and told him I could not live like that any longer. I needed forgiveness for everything I had done wrongfully toward him. And I needed help with getting my mind under control and to take away the guilt and the pain of Terry's death. Life is difficult when you try it on your own we all need a friend. In John 15:13, "Greater love has no one than this, that he lay down his life for his friends." Jesus did that for me.

He did it for you. Jesus is the best friend we could ever hope or ask for. God answered my prayers but it took time and it took help.

At the age of nineteen now I was beginning to cope with the death of my best friend. At this time through some difficulties of her own life, a young gal, Laura had made her way some one thousand miles from her home state of Pennsylvania to my little town in Mississippi. She was working at a local hotel and would come in to buy the groceries for the hotel. We would talk when Laura came into the store. One day I was coached by her friend who was with her to ask her out. I did and she said, "Yes." After the date we talked way into the night. It just felt good to have someone to talk with. It took my mind off the loss of my friend.

A couple weeks later Laura flew home to spend Thanksgiving with her family. I did not want her to go because I thought her family would talk her into staying and I did not want to be alone again. She assured me she would be back so she flew to Pennsylvania for the holiday. A week later she was back.

Genesis 2:18 says, "The Lord God said, It is not good for man to be alone. I will make him a helper suitable for him." God gave Adam a helpmate. He did not want Adam to be alone. And I believe God gave me a helpmate to help me through that difficult time in my life. She confessed to me some time after her return that while she was in Pennsylvania she told her family, "I'm going to marry that guy." And the following February after much debate and begging with her parents and mine, we were married.

Genesis 1:28 says, "God blessed them, and said to them, be fruitful and increase in number; fill the earth and subdue it." And we were fruitful. In December of that year we had our first child, our firstborn, a son we named Matthew. Fourteen months later, not planned but with joy, Nicholas, our second son, was born.

At twenty-two years old the first couple of years we did not go to church much, even though we did talk about church and God. I had been given a job promotion in a different town. We had moved, I think, three times. Our religious backgrounds were somewhat different but we both believed in God and his son Jesus. Laura's family was mostly Episcopalians where I on the other hand was raised Baptist and Presbyterian. We did, however, begin going to a small church in our country community where we lived after Nicholas was born. We attended church regularly. Our lives, like most young couples with children, were very busy.

We lived in a mobile home and wanted more children, so I designed a home for us that I would build in the yard in front of the mobile home. After nine months of working on it every moment we had to spare, it was finished. We were so proud of our house. It turned out very nice. God was blessing my work. Our family, our home, and our church life were grand. A few short months later we had our third child, another son, Levi. Psalm 127:3-4 (KJV) *Lo, children are a heritage of the Lord: and the fruit of the womb is his reward. As arrows are in the hand of a mighty man; so are children of the youth.*

When I built our home, I had taken out a personal loan until after the house was built. Then the bank was going to give us a regular mortgage loan on the house. I borrowed $8,000. The house appraised for $24,000 but when they redid the loan instead of a fifteen or twenty year loan they gave us a seven year loan. My payments were double what they told me they were going to be. So I had to get another job to afford the house payment. Six months went by, I was always tired. We weren't going to church. No time for church, no time for the family, no time for anything but work.

So at the age of twenty-five I had all I could take. I quit both my jobs for a couple of reasons, packed the family up, dropped the house keys at the bank, and left town. We moved to a small house that had belonged to an aunt of mine who had passed away. Rent was only $50 a month, but there was some work that needed done to it. When I went for unemployment they let me know you don't get unemployment if you just quit your job. But we did get food stamps because of the children. Thank goodness we had three kids so we did not go hungry. Laura did get a job at a fast food restaurant but she wasn't making very much. At first we didn't mind it we got by but that's about it. I loved being Mr. Mom. We would get up in the morning, eat, get the work done around the house, and outside we would be the rest of the day. But the fun time wore off pretty quickly. We had been living at that place for about four months. We were always broke. We were not going to church. Laura would ask for money from her folks because my mother and stepdad were as broke as we were, so we couldn't ask them. Finally my wife's father, told us to pack our stuff up and move to Pennsylvania. We talked it over and decided to go. I was getting a check from the grocery store I had worked at for eight years for $3000. It was my retirement fund I could get early. So we took the money rented a hauling truck and moved to Pennsylvania. Between paying bills we had, renting the truck and buying the gas for the trip we arrived in Pennsylvania with only a few dollars left in our pockets. We stayed with my wife's father for awhile until we got on our feet. My father-in-law found me a job within a week. It was a little more than minimum wage but it was a job no less.

We started going where my wife's family went to church. A big Episcopal church in town. It was a different kind of worship than I was used to, let me tell you. Nowhere close to Baptist. But we went every week with her family. Then one day her uncle introduced me to a man at their church who was the president of a heater company. He got me an interview at that company with the personnel manager.

When I went for my interview the personnel manager asked me, "How do you know the president of the company?" I just told him, "Oh I go to church with him." The personnel manager said, "Well, he must like you because you've got the job." Three months after moving to Pennsylvania I had a job that paid me more than both my jobs I had in Mississippi. God was blessing my family and me, no doubt about it.

I was working a lot of overtime. The company was usually busy from September through the first of February. After a few short weeks of overtime I decided I didn't like going to my wife's family church any more. I made excuses: "I'm tired, I don't like it, it is weird." So we stopped going altogether. Shortly after we quit going to church one of my co-workers invited me to share some pot with him after work. Not too long after that I was buying a small bag for myself to use after work. I was on afternoon turn so by the time I got home Laura and the kids were already in bed and sleeping.

By this time I wasn't reading my Bible any longer but I was still praying most nights asking for forgiveness for what I had done that evening. Romans 8:5 says, "Those who live according to the sinful nature have their minds set on what that nature desires; but those who live in accordance with the Spirit have their minds set on what the Spirit desires." I had let my sinful nature over take my spiritual nature. I had dropped my guard; I had given sin a foot in the door and it was beginning to open the door up even further.

I only bought pot for a few months. I was too scared, too nervous. I thought for sure the cops were watching me everywhere I went. So I started drinking alcohol instead. At least that was legal, and I didn't have to worry about going to jail for drinking. At that time in my life I thought I had everything under control. I had a nice family, good place to live, made good money. Life was ok.

But something had happened during that part of my life that I hadn't even realized. Not only were we not going to church, I was not reading my Bible anymore, and I had completely stopped praying altogether. I was living a selfish life. Look at me; look what I have done. I didn't need God. I was doing just fine by myself.

It reminds me of a story about king Nebuchadnezzar in the Old Testament book of Daniel chapter 4. As Nebuchadnezzar stood up on the rooftop of his royal palace he said, in verse 30, "Is this not the great Babylon I have built as the royal residence, by my mighty power and for the glory of my majesty?" Then in verses 31-32 it says, "This is what is decreed for you, King Nebuchadnezzar: Your royal authority has been taken from you. You will be driven away from people and will live with the wild animals; you will eat grass like cattle." After a time set by God the Bible says that Nebuchadnezzar raised his head toward heaven and his sanity was restored and he praised, honored and glorified God.

I was so self-centered at that time I didn't even recognize my own destruction. One night after work I went home to find myself once again alone and by myself. Everyone was already in bed by the time I had gotten home. I stood at the kitchen sink, poured a fifth of bourbon in a quart jar, and drank it right down before I left the kitchen. I went into the living room and sat down to watch TV. In a short period of time my head was spinning. I staggered over to a bed we had set up in the living room and laid down. I laid there thinking, *Man, am I sick. What did I do that for?* Then I felt it coming back up. I leaned over the edge of the bed and threw up. What a mess. I laid there a couple of minutes, got sick to my stomach again, leaned over to throw up and fell out of the bed into my own vomit. I was so sick I just laid there. After a while I somehow managed to pull myself back into that bed and sleep it off.

I survived that night and stopped drinking. I know if I had not thrown up as soon as I did that night and the rest of that fifth of alcohol had got into my blood steam I probably would have died.

The next day I had a lot of cleaning up to do. Myself, the bed, the floor, all of it I cleaned up. Physically cleaned up, that is, but what I needed was a spiritual cleaning. I was so far backslidden, I was so far from God, I was so much in the dark I couldn't see. I had taken myself so far away from God that there was nothing but darkness. I was spiritually blind walking in darkness.

Not too long after the drinking episode sometime during the night I dreamed of a beautiful blue sky with puffy white clouds when all of a sudden from the clouds came these words. "Come back to me or I will bring you home." I cannot put into words the power or the authority of that voice I heard, but I immediately woke up: I was shaking, sweating, and very scared. I asked God then and there to please forgive me and he did. I felt like the prodigal son coming home after wallowing around in the pig pens of the world. And just like the father in the parable opened up his arms and welcomed his son back to him, so my Father in heaven welcomed me back into his arms, back into fellowship with him. I told Laura about my dream and the following Sunday we found a Baptist church nearby and began attending every week. I began reading my Bible again, and praying every day. Trying to put my spiritual life back into some kind of order. The joy of the Lord was in my life. Not only that, but the joy of fatherhood once again returned to me.

Chapter Two

At the age of twenty-seven we had our fourth child, a daughter, finally. Sarah, daddy's little princess. Now the people I worked with had begun noticing a change in me. I was smiling a lot, humming a lot, meditating on the word. Ephesians 5:19 (KJV) *Speaking to yourselves in psalms and hymns and spiritual songs, singing and making melody in your heart to the Lord.* And that's just what I did. I would be at work singing to the Lord, making up songs to the Lord. I didn't know how to read or write music. I would just make up the tune in my head. Here is the first song I wrote.

Jesus my savior, he is my best friend. Jesus my savior, he you can always depend. Jesus my savior, would you let him come in? Into your heart and make you whole. Would you let him come in?

When you walk with Christ our Lord, you can always fill joy. When you work for Christ our Lord, you he will always employ. When you talk to Christ our Lord, he will always be there. Talk to the Lord and let him in, into your heart today.

Oh precious Father, you gave us your only son. Oh precious Father, he is the only one. Oh precious Father, through him hearts could be right. He paid it all too all that receive, the gift of eternal life.

Oh heavenly Father, with you there is no doubt. Oh heavenly Father, how can they live without? Oh heavenly Father, they want to be saved. Raise up your heads and give him praise, for saving your soul today. Lift up your heads and give God praise for saving your soul today.

In a matter of weeks after my dream of God calling me back into his fellowship, I had another dream. This time I was standing in front of a large group of people in a white suit and I had long hair, telling the people in the dream about Jesus. I woke up from the dream not sweating this time, not in fear this time, but very nervous, having questions I needed answered. Was this a dream from God? Was this a dream of my own? Was this a dream of my own imagination? After praying and asking God for guidance, I was convinced it was from God. I told my wife and she believed it was from God also. So we continued to go to church each week and I let my hair begin to grow. Continuing in the word and waiting on the Lord to see where he was leading me.

Once a month our church had church services at a local nursing home for the residence there. We would go to their rooms and ask if they wanted to come to the service. If the answer was yes we would help them to the lounge. We would sing a few hymns and then someone would give a short talk. That was a ministry my wife and I both enjoyed.

I was feeling confident in my walk by this time and trying to trust in the Lord to the best of my ability. I decided I wanted to join the choir at church so I told the pastor one day after the church service. He told me sorry but my hair was too long to be in the choir. By this time it was barely touching my collar. I was shocked that I was told no. So I went home, prayed about it and left it up to the Lord. After that it seemed like every week the pastor would have a comment about my hair. He would tell me after church don't you think you should cut your hair. You can't sing in the choir with that long hair. Or he would say the Bible says a man should have short hair it is a disgrace for a man to have long hair. I just ignored him and thought to myself all the pictures of Jesus he has long hair, I had remembered reading about Samson he had long hair, and the prophet Samuel both of these men had long hair because the Bible said no razor was to touch their heads. So I was confused.

One day the pastor told me that in the book of 1 Corinthians it said if a man had long hair it was disgrace. So I went home and read my Bible until I found what he was talking about. 1 Corinthians 11:14, "Does not the very nature of things teach you that if a man has long hair, it is a disgrace to him." Well, there it was in the Bible just like the pastor said. Now I had a battle going on in my head. Was I supposed to cut my hair and sing in the choir? Was the dream I had with long hair and telling people about Jesus not from God after all? God would not tell me to do something that was against his inspired word in the Bible.

One evening after a few weeks of praying and agonizing over my problem I was sitting at the dining room table. In an almost last resort on my part I asked God if he would please just give me a sign or something if he wanted me to continue with the long hair. I was not only having problems from the pastor, but now my wife wasn't really liking it much either. I sat there for a while reading the word and nothing jump out at me from the Bible. In my frustration, I finally cried out in an arrogant and demanding shout, "I need a sign and I need a sign from you now, Lord." And did I ever get one. Lightning hit just outside our mobile home! My heart was pounding in my chest and immediately Matthew 4:7 (KJV) *Thou shalt not tempt the Lord thy God* came to mind.

Laura came from the back of the house asking, "What was that? I felt the house shake." The lights were out and I told her that lightning had hit outside. We went outside to look with a flashlight and the underneath of the mobile home was on fire. We called the fire department. While waiting on them to arrive, I tried to put flour on it because with the power out, the water pump wouldn't work. The fire department came, finished putting out the fire, and the power came back on shortly after.

After all the commotion I sat down, asked for forgiveness and left my hair alone. Thank goodness he is a forgiving and loving God.

At the age of twenty-eight we moved again and we were about fifteen miles from where we were attending church. So we decided it was too far to drive and stopped going. I slowly started drifting backwards once again. I cut my hair and I stopped studying my Bible. I still read it but I wasn't looking for guidance. Still prayed but not for guidance.

I bought an old car, a 1971 Pontiac LeMans. It had a 455 police interceptor motor and a Muncie 4 speed tranny. But the body was shot. That car was fast, let me tell ya. It was so rusty, though, the trunk bottom was gone. You opened up the trunk lid and you could see the gas tank. So I spent evenings and Sundays working on that car. I learned how to do body work by teaching myself. After a few weeks the outside of the car was done. I put a double layer of cardboard in the trunk, duct taped it down, and sprayed car undercoating on top of the cardboard. After that the gaskets behind the exhaust manifold were leaking, so I had to replace them.

One weekend I put the car up on ramps and blocked the back wheels so I could replaced the gaskets and put on new headers. One thing I had to do was unhook the clutch linkage to put the new headers on. After replacing everything I removed the blocks, got into the car, and took it for a spin. The new headers sounded great but at high rpm's the clutch was slipping, so I put the car back on the ramps. I slid underneath the car and began to adjust the clutch. Only one problem: I adjusted it the wrong way.

All of a sudden the clutch let loose and the car rolled down the ramps. I had forgotten to replace the blocks behind the wheels. On the way down the ramps, a bolt underneath the frame caught hold of my shirt sleeve and turned me on my side, and then the car stopped. Now here I was, pinned under the car kicking my feet and screaming the best I could, but hardly any sound was coming out. Laura looked out the window, saw the car was not on the ramp and saw my feet kicking. She called for an ambulance right away. By the time she made it out to check on me I had managed to get turned on my back and lifted the car up far enough for me to get out.

When the ambulance arrived I could hardly talk my mouth was bloody from me biting my tongue. They first thought I had internal injuries. After checking me out they transported me to the hospital. Lots of X-rays were taken, with no broken bones found thank you, Jesus. I was bruised and very sore. I was off work for a week. Later on I measured the distance from the frame of the car to the ground it was only 8 1/4 inches. With God's intervention I survived the car rolling on top of me with only minor injuries.

At this time of my life I was riding with Clara, a woman I worked with who had become my unofficial adopted mom. My mother was one thousand miles south in Mississippi so Clara was my northern mom. She had come by to check on me while I was off work. On returning to work we would meet between our two homes. I would leave my car at a store parking lot. Then I would drive her car to work. She is a very devoted Christian woman. We would talk about God and other things with each other. I didn't share too much personal testimony about my walk, mostly general stuff, because I wasn't walking with God at that time in my life. I was doing things in my life that I knew I should not have been doing, but did them anyway.

One morning I left my home to meet Clara for our ride to work when all of a sudden an animal ran out in front of me. I jerked the car to the right. The right hand side of the front bumper dug into a dirt bank. The back end of the car slid forward. Then the car rolled over on its roof. When it came to a stop I was upside down sideways in the middle of the road. The top was crushed in the front part of the car. The doors were crushed and jammed. The back window was broken out. I managed to crawl out where the back window was supposed to be.

I was standing there leaning against the back of the car, trying to get myself together, when Clara drove up. She came to check on me because I didn't show up at our meeting place. She just thought I had overslept. She went and called for a wrecker for me, then went on to work. She picked me up for work until we got another car.

But I will never forget that next day when we were on our way to work she gave me a brief talk. She said to me, "I don't know what you have done or what you are doing, but you better stop and get right with the Lord. He will forgive you, just ask." 1 John 1:9 says (KJV) *If we confess our sins, he is faithful and just to forgive us our sins.* And no matter how many times we mess up when we come to him and ask for forgiveness he will forgive us. In Matthew 18:21-22, "Then Peter came to Jesus and asked, "Lord, how many times shall I forgive my brother when he sins against me? Up to seven times?" Jesus answered, "I tell you not seven times but seventy-seven times." Well, I took her advice, asked God to forgive me, and to help me to live a life for him.

When I was twenty-nine we went back to church, but this time we went to a Nazarene Church. Now it was different from the

Baptist. They taught more on sanctification and living a holy life for God. Not that the Baptist doesn't teach on holy living; it just wasn't the same emphasis as the Nazarene church. We met some good people at the Nazarene church and they loved the Lord. I began not just reading my Bible but studying it a lot at that time because of the differences between the Baptist and the Nazarene churches. We went to both Sunday school and church services at the Nazarene church. Up until that point we had just been going to the church services. Both my wife and I and the children liked Sunday school. We liked the songs at the Nazarene church. The hymns were different from the Baptist ones, but very good. Every month that had five Sundays in them, that Sunday evening service became a special singing service. Quite often they would have special guest singers come to the church. Life was good; life was very good. Work was good, family was good, church was good, and we had moved once again, this time to our own house.

We had found a fixer upper. I remember the first time I looked at the house. I walked in the back door, made a trip through the house, and went right back out to our car. The house had holes in the walls, smelled like cats, had cat litter on the floor in the dining room and the outside of the house needed redone. It needed more work than I wanted to do but, my wife talked me into buying it. After a couple of months of working on it in my spare time, we moved into our own home. Hallelujah! After moving every year for the past three years we now had a home.

We continued going to the Nazarene church. I was studying my Bible a lot searching for answers to the questions I had between the doctrines of the two different denominations. I believe God used that time in my life not for me to just read the Bible but for studying the Bible for seeking out answers. In Acts 17:11, "Now the Bereans were of more noble character than the Thessalonians, for they received the message with great eagerness and examined the Scriptures every day to see if what Paul said was true." We need to be in the word of God every day to make sure of what we are being taught.

We had made good friends at the Nazarene church but the church was moving to a new location. We visited a couple of Baptist churches that were within five miles of our home. We decided on a Baptist church next to the children's school. It wasn't long before we felt right at home there. The people were friendly. They had good Sunday school classes for the children and the adults. They had Boy Scout and Cub Scout meetings at the church. My oldest two boys were interested in becoming Cub Scouts. We joined the church.

I met with the pastor and shared with him about my conversion, my two divine dreams I had received and my life's story. He told me that if God had a call on my life to preach that I needed to seek it out and let God's will be done. So he took me under his wing and gave me use of his entire library of study books. We got in touch with our regional Baptist minister. The pastor and I met with the area minister. He wanted me to go to a lay minister's school. I checked out the info it sounded great only I had one problem. It was on Saturdays and I could not get that day off from work. So I just kept studying on my own with books the pastor would lend me. One day I was watching a well known pastor on TV who had a college Bible course you could take at home. I was so excited I called for the info. After I looked it over I talk to my wife and then the pastor about the course. He really wanted me to take the other course offered by the Baptist association. But my hands were tied. I could not get off every Saturday for schooling. So the pastor agreed this was the best thing for me at that time. The course was from a well-known Baptist college.

At the age of thirty I was loving life. The Bible course had arrived and I was just so excited about it. I was studying it every chance I had. I would get up an hour, hour and a half before I had to leave for work to study and any other spare time I could find. I would take my test for the week on Sunday afternoons. My grades were mostly A's and a couple of B's. I had decided to stop chewing tobacco which I had been doing since I was fifteen years old. I was sharing the gospel with people at work. The Holy Spirit was helping me every day. I would ask the Holy Spirit to give me the strength, the ability, and the courage to share with my co-workers every day. I convinced a group of Christians to come together before our shift started each day for a time of sharing and prayer. That was an awesome time. We would lift each other up, and we would lift up our supervisors and all the leaders of our company in prayer that they would make good decisions throughout the day.

I was also writing more songs and poems during this time of my life. Here is one of the poems I wrote.

No Pain No Gain

My Savior died on Calvary
he shed his blood for you and me.
My savior suffered upon that tree
long, long ago at Calvary.
Try and think about the pain
my savior endured that we might gain.
The life eternal, with him someday
for that was the price he had to pay.
They nailed him up and mocked his name
but Jesus loved them just the same.
His love for us is mighty and great
that's why he died for our sake.
So think if you will about my friend
if you're still living in a life of sin.
Jesus gave his life for you and for me

so we could have life with him eternally.
If you want to know deep inside
how he gave his blood and suffered and died.
Go to the cross and share in the pain
then you will receive what he wanted you to gain.

At the age of thirty-one the time had finally came for me to see if I could do what I believed in my heart God had called me to do. The pastor was going on vacation. He ask me if I was ready to give the message to the congregation on Sunday morning. I felt like I was and told the pastor yes. He said, "Okay, I will leave the preaching up to you. One of the Deacons will do the announcements, the prayer; that sort of thing so you don't have to worry about them."

Well that was a relief. I was already nervous just agreeing to do the message. He gave me a three week notice, thank goodness. I needed every minute of it. I prayed about the message and God answered my prayer. I had the title of my sermon right away "Listening, Trusting and Obeying God." Now I just had to put all the other pieces together. I picked out three hymns. *Living for Jesus, Trust and Obey.* and *I Surrender All.* Then I spent the next three weeks preparing my sermon.

I had the dining room table filled with books. That was way before I had a personal computer like these days. I had three different Bible versions, I had two different concordances, a Bible dictionary, and a couple of Bible commentaries. The Scripture reading I chose was from 1 Samuel 3:1-10. These Bible verses tell of the young boy Samuel who would grow up to become a prophet of God. Samuel's mentor was the prophet Eli. Eli helped Samuel to recognize the call of the Lord and told Samuel to answer the Lord and to listen to what the Lord had to say to him.

Unlike in the days of the Old Testament when God spoke through a select few persons, Jesus says in John 10-27, "My sheep listen to my voice; I know them, and they follow me." Nowadays with the new covenant in effect, any child of God can hear from the Lord. No special privileges to only a select few. But just like Samuel, we have to learn to listen to the voice of the Lord. This world is so fast paced we just have to slow down sometimes, be still, and listen for the voice of the Lord. Then when the Lord tells us to do something, we should trust him and obey him. That's what my first sermon was about. These words are still true even today. I was encouraged by the church that day in my first attempt at serving the Lord by preaching the word of God. I was having a mountaintop experience in what I had accomplished through the help of the Holy Spirit. I had been so nervous, but when it was over I knew my Father in heaven was proud of me. Not that I had given one of the greatest sermons that Sunday, but that I had trusted God and did what I believed he wanted me to do.

But then things changed. Not long after my first sermon my wife broke some news to me. She told me she did not want to be a preacher's wife. I told her it's not like I am going to be a pastor of a church, nothing like that I just believed God had called me to be an evangelist. I believed God would have me visit other churches and help spread the good news. The good news of who Jesus was and what he has done for me, what he has done for all who believe.

Well that did not satisfy her, living the life of a preacher's wife or an evangelist's wife, whichever one it would be too demanding, too confining, too religious. She felt like she would be under a microscope for everyone to look at, and compare her life to. That was just too much for her to undertake. So I packed away all of my college study material and put them in the closet on hold for a while.

My wife worked at a group home with mentally challenged people. On every other Sunday she would bring them to church, but that stopped. After that she stopped going to church altogether.

She didn't like my long hair anymore, so I cut it off. Finally we just were not happy any longer. I was nineteen and she was sixteen when we got married. Now at thirty-two and twenty-nine our lives were so different from anything we had ever dreamed or planned.

I arranged for one week off of work to go back to Mississippi. I packed our two youngest children's clothes, our son Levi and our daughter Sarah, then clothes for myself and headed back home to Mississippi. Upon arriving I made arrangements to stay with my sister, Brenda and her family. Then I went to visit my mother. I talked to her about my problems.

I decided to go see my former meat market supervisor who had jurisdiction over the grocery stores I had worked at before moving to Pennsylvania. I called and made an appointment to meet with him on a Monday.

Now we had showed up unexpectedly. I had surprised everyone, not only with my problems but with the visit. Easter weekend was coming up. I hadn't thought at all about that. But my sister, who worked at a florist, had been making Easter baskets inside large balloons that year. She made Sarah and Levi two nice baskets for Easter Sunday. We went to church with my family that Easter Sunday and Sarah and Levi were shocked that the Easter bunny had found them in Mississippi, so far from our home in Pennsylvania.

I went to my appointment. I told my former supervisor that I had been living in Pennsylvania for the last five years but would like to move back to Mississippi. I asked if he had any meat market openings available; meat cutter, meat wrapper, anything at all. He told me if I had been there a week earlier, he would not only have had an opening, but I could have had my old job back. Not just a meat cutter but assistant market manager could have been mine for the taking. He told me how good it was to see me. That he would check to see if he could find me an opening in one of his stores. I told him I only had a week then I would have to go back to Pennsylvania. He said for me to call him back on Friday to see what he had come up with.

I spent the next few days with my family. I went to visit my father and stepmom during that week. I wanted to see if my father could give me some advice on my situation. After our visit I took all my father's advice into consideration. I also did a lot of thinking and praying, asking God what I should do. Should I stay and try to find a job? But if I did that, what about my other two children in Pennsylvania? When would I ever see them again? I was confused, unsure of what to do. I just told God if he wanted me to stay in Mississippi, then when I called my former supervisor he would have an opening for me. And if there were no job openings, back to Pennsylvania I would go. In my mind I had left my future in God's hands. In the gospel of John 14:1, Jesus comforting his disciples before he was arrested said these words to them, "Do not let your hearts be troubled. Trust in God; trust also in me."

On Friday I called my former supervisor. He said I have looked, and I have searched, and I have tried to come up with some kind of a job for you but I just do not have anything open right now. I thanked him for everything and hung up the phone. It was time to head back north. I visited with my family the rest of that day. Then I packed our clothes. We would head out in the morning. My family and I cried, said our goodbyes, and we headed home.

Upon arriving home I had so missed my other two children Matthew and Nicholas and even my wife. We talked for a while, trying to find a solution to our problems. We came up with a plan over the next few days to try to make the marriage work. I continued to go to church with the children but Laura just worked. She would not come. My Sunday school class prayed for us. Our pastor not only prayed but also offered marriage counseling for us but Laura didn't want anyone knowing about our problems. So instead of getting help, we just continued going downhill, until at last we just gave up on ever being happy again. We had decided to split up on the Fourth of July, Independence Day. I kept our house. Our two youngest children our daughter Sarah and our son Levi were to stay with me. I also kept my work car for our transportation. Laura took the new van we had only purchased a few months earlier. Neither of us could afford both payments on the house and the new van. So I took the house that way I didn't have to up root the two youngest children. My wife needed reliable transportation; she had just finished LPN nursing school and had to travel a good distance to take her state exams, plus she would be going for job interviews.

My wife and my two oldest sons Matthew and Nicholas moved in with her sister, who had also finished nursing school too. My life was hard, my life was tough, my life stunk. Here I was trying to raise a four year old daughter and a seven year old son on my own. Get up early enough to get myself and two kids ready, drive them fifteen miles to the sitter and then drive another fifteen miles to my job. Work eight hours pick them up from the sitter and then drive home. Try to figure out something for us to eat, try to spend some time with them. Also doing dishes, taking baths, doing laundry, just normal household stuff. By the time the kids went to bed at night I was exhausted, flat give out.

I would crawl in bed but not be able to go to sleep. I would lie there and try to figure out where I had gone wrong, what I could have done differently. I just felt so alone in the world especially at night while lying in bed. I had shared my bed with my wife for almost fourteen years and now I was alone. I felt empty. Each passing day that went by it seemed to get worse and worse and worse.

I was falling into a deep depression, but I tried not to show it. I could hardly keep up with everything I had to get done in a day.

I actually liked the daytime when I was so busy I didn't have time to think about my problems, but at night they would just bombard my mind.

I was still going to church with my two kids, being encouraged each week by the pastor and my Sunday school class. I was no longer seeking God on my own. I had stopped reading the Bible. I didn't have time, I still prayed, but I didn't believe God was listening to me. My prayers were not getting answered the way I wanted them to be answered. So I didn't pray as much as I had before. No I was slowly pulling away from God personally. And because I did not believe God was listening to me, I thought God must not care for me anymore.

Finally I had convinced myself that God was so angry at me that he did not care what happened to me at all. I had let my own mind, all of my negative thinking, all of my negative thoughts, put there by either Satan or one of his demonic helpers, convince me that I was no longer able to be a husband, a father, a provider for my family (what was left of it), a Christian, or even a human being. I was so useless to this world as a person that this world would not miss me at all if I was not here. I was a loser in this life, a loser in this world, a loser with a capital L. And as time went by I started contemplating suicide. I would think about how I would do it. What should I do with the kids? Would I write a letter? But why would I write a letter; no one would care what I had to say. Over and over I would think upon these things in my mind.

In Genesis chapter 4 we have the story of Cain and Abel. Beginning with the second half of verse 2-7, "Now Abel kept flocks, and Cain worked the soil. In the course of time Cain brought some of the fruits of the soil as an offering to the Lord. But Abel brought fat portions from some of the firstborn of his flock. The Lord looked with favor on Abel and his offering, but on Cain and his offering he did not look with favor. So Cain was very angry, and his face was downcast. Then the Lord said to Cain, "Why are you angry? Why is your face downcast? If you do what is right, will you not be accepted? But if you do not do what is right, sin is crouching at your door; it desires to have you, but you must master it."

I'm sure most of us have heard the story of Cain and Abel but what I think we often miss from these verses is that God gave Cain a warning of what would happen if he did not rethink his situation he was in. God was telling him that he needed to change the way he was thinking or something worse was going to happen, something worse other than the way he felt. But Cain did not listen to God. He gave in to the temptation of sin, the temptation that Satan most likely kept bombarding Cain with. Until Cain killed his own brother Abel, the first recorded murder in the Bible.

And just like Cain I gave into temptation and decided to end it all. I just could not take it any longer. In August just one month after our separation I made plans for Laura to keep Sarah and Levi overnight.

I stopped by a store in town and picked up several over-the-counter medicines to take. I had picked up some cold medicine, some antihistamines, and sleeping tablets. I looked for medicines that would cause heart failure if you took too many. I figured that way I would have a heart attack in my sleep and that would be it. I would not leave a note. That way if I died of a heart attack my wife would get our insurance money to help with the children. Do you see how delusional Satan can make a person? I never thought about them doing an autopsy on me after I died and finding all the medication in my blood. But I took over one hundred pills laid down on the bed and waited for death to come.

After a while I began to feel some effects of the medicines I had taken. I just remember feeling faint, weak, and it seemed like my heart was pounding a mile a minute. And then I began to cry.

What had I done? I began thinking about my children, Matthew, Nicholas, Levi, and Sarah, one by one, how much I loved them, how precious each one of them was to me. How would they ever forgive me for leaving them and how would it affect their lives?

I cried out to God. I told him how sorry I was for being such a failure in this world, but most of all a failure at being one of his children. Then I asked my Father in heaven to help me. First and foremost, would he please forgive me for what I had done for taking all those pills? Then I asked if he would have mercy on me and let me live. And if he did let me live, would he please help me cope with the pain and the guilt I was trying to endure by myself? I rolled over as I was crying out to God and went to sleep.

A couple of hours went by and I woke up. I had not died. God had mercy on me. I thanked God for giving me another chance for life here on this earth. I felt fine. No side effects. I was hungry. So I got up went to town and had something to eat. I came back home and watched TV for awhile. I talked to my Father in heaven, thanking him again for saving my life. It is hard for us sometimes as human beings to comprehend how much God loves us. Romans 8:38-39, "For I am convinced that neither death nor life, neither angels nor demons, neither the present nor the future, nor any powers, neither height nor depth, nor anything else in all creation, will be able to separate us from the love of God that is in Christ Jesus our Lord." Amen and Amen to that. The next day I picked up my kids and life carried on.

Chapter Three

On Sunday my two kids and I went to church. After Sunday school one of the ladies in my class, Diana, slipped me a note and told me to read it when I got home. I said ok and slipped it into my Bible to read later. After I got home I opened up the note to see what it said. It read, "If you need someone to talk with, someone to help with the children, or if you need help doing house work call me at 555-123-4567. Your Christian friend Diana."

First of all, I was shocked that she would want to bother talking to me about my problems, although she was in my Sunday school class. But she also offered to help with my children, and with the house work. I thought, *this is strange, are my kids and I her charity work?* I just really didn't know what to think, so I waited a couple of days and called her on the phone. I told her I had read the note after church. I was just calling to thank her for her offer. If I needed to talk I would give her a call.

The next Sunday Sarah, Levi, and I went to Sunday school and church as usual. After church Diana came up to say hi to the kids,

I had already seen her in Sunday school. She knelt down and asked the kids, "What are you going to do today?" I had already made plans to take my kids to the movies after lunch. So they told her, "We are going to the movies."

"What movie are you going to see?" she asked.

They yelled, "*The Duck Tale Movie Treasure of the Lost Lamp.*" They had seen the advertisements for it on TV for a couple of weeks.

Diana said, "That sounds like a good movie to go see."

Well, I just looked at her and asked, "Do you want to go with us?"

She smiled and said, "Yes I would." So I told her I would pick her up sometime after lunch when I found out what time the afternoon movie started.

Sarah, Levi, and I picked up Diana and headed to the movies. We arrived at the theater, got our tickets, pop and popcorn, and went in to watch the movie. We had a good time.

Diana got a little workout with Sarah. After Sarah drank all her pop she had to go to the bathroom. So Diana asked, "I can take her if you want?"

I ask, "Are you sure?"

She said, "Yes, I'll take her."

I answered, "Thanks," and off they went. They returned shortly thereafter, but ten minutes later Sarah had to go again. So Diana took her again and then again. The last half-hour of the movie they spent going back and forth to the bathroom.

The movie was over we left for home. I thanked Diana for going with us and dropped her off at her house. Then my kids and I headed home. That had been a refreshing afternoon; the kids had fun, I had fun, and I thought Diana had fun too. Later on that evening I called her up. I thanked her for going and helping with the children. She said she was happy to do it and if I needed anything do not hesitate to call. We said goodnight to each other and I hung up the phone.

The next week there was going to be a local fair we have in our hometown every year. So I called Diana to see if she would go with my kids and me to the fair. Diana agreed to go, so we picked her up and headed to the fair. Diana was really good with the kids and they seemed to take a liking to her. We walked around the fairground with the kids and looked at the farm animals. We looked at all the different things people entered the fair for ribbons. Arts and Crafts, Fresh Vegetables, Canned Fruits and Vegetables, Cakes, Cookies just to name a few. While walking around the fairground we ran into our pastor and his wife. The pastor said hello to us, then asked if we were enjoying the fair. We said, "Yes," and that was about it. We went on our way.

The next day I got a phone call from the pastor wanting to talk with Diana and me at the church. So Diana and I met with the pastor. During this meeting we found out that we should not go out in public together by ourselves any more. No matter how innocent and harmless we had made it, the fact was I was still married. I was not divorced so he did not want us to be seen in public together. We were allowed to do church activities together. The children and I were allowed to go visit Diana at her house, where she lived with her mother and father, but only once a week on Saturday evenings. She was not allowed to come to my house until I was legally divorced. We were allowed to talk on the phone all we wanted. Now I was just so happy to have someone to talk to, someone that helped brighten up my days, that I was almost beside myself. I was still in shock that there was someone who wanted to spend time with my kids and me. I knew that God loved my kids and me, but I didn't think anyone else would ever really care about us. I believed that Sarah, Levi, and I would just make it through life hanging on to each other.

Just when we least expect it God just does something amazing in our lives. God knew how lonely I was. He knew how helpless I felt, and he brought Diana into my life at just the right time for me. Not the right time for some folks maybe, like Diana's mother and father but just the right time for me. They were having a hard time with our new relationship because I was not divorced yet. I had filed for a divorce but it was not finalized yet. They did not approve of their daughter seeing a married man. So we worked through it the best we could. The kids helped me out with Diana's mother. When we would go over on Saturday nights Diana and her mother would play with the kids. But her father just wasn't having anything to do with the whole situation. I would sit there and try to imagine just what he might say to me if he told me what he was thinking when we came to visit. But as time went by he seemed to soften up, not much, but a little. In September I had filed for the divorce with my ex-wife taking custody of the two oldest children and me the two youngest children. But about the third week in September Nicholas, our second oldest son, wanted to move back in with me. So we had the divorce papers changed. Now I had three kids to raise. I was a busy man but talking to Diana after the kids went to bed at night just helped me make it through those first few months.

In December the divorce was final. No more just seeing Diana at church, no more just seeing Diana at her mother and father's house on Saturday nights, no more just talking to her on the phone at night now she could come over to visit. And that's just what she did; Diana would come over about three times a week. We would play with the kids, and do other fun things like fold the clothes and do the dishes. Then the kids would go to bed and we would have time to spend together, alone time. We would sit and snuggle in the chair and try to watch TV. But we spent most of the time either talking or making funny faces at each other. I was so happy it's hard to believe that just four months earlier I had given up and wanted to end my own life. But that's just what Satan wants us to believe. He wants us to concentrate on everything in a negative way with no possible hope in the future. In the first part of John 10:10 (KJV) *"The thief cometh not, but for to steal, and to kill, and to destroy."* Satan wants to destroy us and it does not matter to him how he does it. But the second part of John 10:10 (KJV) *"I am come that they might have life, and that they might have it more abundantly."* Jesus came to give us an abundant life and Satan comes to destroy our life.

I stopped by to visit Diana's mother and father. I asked them if I could have permission to ask Diana to marry me. They did not want us to get married right away, but they told me I could ask her. Diana's mother gave me one of her rings out of her jewelry box so I knew what size ring to buy. I took the ring I had borrowed back to her mother and father while Diana was at work. I told them I was going to give Diana her engagement ring on Christmas morning. I asked them if they wanted to be there when I gave it to her. They said, "Yes."

On Christmas morning Diana and her parents showed up around 6:00 a.m. We let the children look in their stockings, then they opened their presents. While the children were playing with their new presents, I found one last gift that had Diana's name on it. I had put the ring box inside of a larger box so she did not suspect anything. She opened up the smaller box and saw the ring. Diana looked at me; I asked her if she would marry me. She said, "Yes." Diana and her mother both began to cry; her father gave her a hug, shook my hand then said congratulations to us both.

Diana and I wanted to get married in March but her parents talked us into waiting until May. There was a lot of planning to be done, so we decided on May 18, 1991. Before we knew it the wedding day had arrived. By that time I was well accepted by Diana's whole family. The children stayed with Diana's family while we went to Niagara Falls for our honeymoon. We had a wonderful honeymoon.

We returned home to begin our lives together. There were adjustments to be made but the whole family, adults and children worked hard to become a family. The first big test came only a few short weeks later. Our youngest son fell off a swing at the sitter's house. He broke his wrist on one arm and on the other arm his wrist and forearm were broken. So Levi had a cast on both arms. I had to go on a trip for work, and I would be gone for a week. Diana would have to manage the household on her own after only being married for about six weeks.

She pulled it off with only one small setback. At seven years of age Levi couldn't take a bath with his cast on, but he did not want Diana to see him naked. So Diana had to try and cover her eyes while giving Levi a bath. I called home every night while I was away to talk to my family. They all got along just fine. I was very proud of my new bride. Diana had gone from being a single woman to becoming a wife and a mom of three very well. The children had gone from having a full time father and a part time mother. To having a full time father, a full time mom, and a part time mother. The children adjusted to our blended family very well, I believe.

By the time I was thirty-four Diana and I had been married for about a year and life was good. We were going to church every week. I was now teaching an adult Sunday school class which I had taken over after our previous teacher remarried and moved away. I felt inadequate at first because some of the adults in the class were several years older and (I was sure) a lot wiser than myself. But they wanted me to be the teacher so I accepted the challenge. Now there were adults from eighteen to seventy years old in the class. With the help of the Holy Spirit we learned a lot from each other.

I shared with Diana the dream I had about preaching, having long hair and my college Bible course. Diana agreed that I should begin my studies again. If I felt God wanted me to have long hair she had no problem with letting it grow. So that's just what I did. The hair began to grow and so did I in my studies. Now I just had to try and figure out how to do everything so I didn't get anything off balance. Diana and I both work all day; since I got home first I did the cooking. After supper Diana did the dishes and we spent time doing family things together. First a devotional time of reading and prayer then playing games inside or outside depending on the weather. Then Diana and the children would watch some TV while I studied. Then off to bed for the children, then Diana and I had some alone time. As time went by I was asked to be a deacon at our church. I was surprised and honored both, by the invitation. I was much younger than all the other deacons. But I accepted and in doing that whenever the pastor would take a Sunday off or go on vacation he would have me fill in for him.

So for the next couple of years I preached some half a dozen times. He always gave me about three weeks notice because he knew I liked a lot of time for preparation. I would just pray and ask God what would he like for me to talk about this time and I would go from there. Three of my sermon titles were "Friend or Enemy, who would you rather spend eternity with? What must I do to enter the Kingdom of God? and Seek ye first the Kingdom of God and his righteousness." Do you see the connection here? I just wanted other people to know God the Father, to know his son Jesus, and to know the Holy Spirit, and how they can change lives.

About this time the members of our church decided to have a mini-revival. Three nights of singing, praying, and worshiping God together with our community and anyone else who would come. The church made up flyers and passed them out. The church wanted three different speakers, one for each night. I volunteered myself for one night and asked if I could call upon a couple of other men I worked with, to fill in the other two nights. The church board that was heading up the mini-revival agreed. They liked the idea of local men of God speaking to our community instead of getting someone to come in from far away. And we were not concerned about what denomination the other speakers served in either.

The one speaker was the pastor of a small church who just happened to work full time with me at the factory. Bill was a great man of God who I believe loved the Lord with all his heart. He agreed to speak one night of the revival. The other speaker I asked was Terry, another co-worker of mine at the factory. He also agreed to speak at the mini-revival.

The three nights of the revival were refreshing, were uplifting, were family of God oneness for those three nights in our little community Baptist church. We preached on love for our community, love for one another, and the love of God. All three nights were uplifting for everyone who attended.

Though we had many talks at work about God and his amazing love, it was great listening to my co-workers preaching from the pulpit. And both sermons touched my heart and the hearts of those in attendance. But the night Terry came to preach he brought along the youth choir from his church. Terry was an African American and I had personally never been to an African American church before. Those young people sang their hearts out, they moved with the music, they clapped their hands, they loved singing about the Lord.

When the third night was over, you could tell that God had blessed everyone who attended the services that week. What a time of sharing, a time of growing and a time of loving in the Lord. In John 17:20-21, Jesus praying for believers says, "My prayer is not for them alone. I pray also for those who will believe in me through their message, that all of them may be one, Father, just as you are in me and I am in you. May they also be in us so that the world may believe that you have sent me?" At that time, at that place, in that little community. We had broken the racial barrier; we had broken the denominational barrier between us as believers in Jesus. We had become one with each other, one with our Father in heaven, and one with Jesus. A few weeks after the revival Terry was ordained at his home church for ministry. Diana and I both attended the ceremony.

In James 4:8, "Come near to God and he will come near to you." I had finally came to a place in my relationship where I was not just loving God, not just serving God, not just living for God, and not just praying to God, but I also began having conversations with God. God would actually talk to me. I have heard people say, "God told me this," or, "God told me to do that." And I had believed they just meant they had a feeling or they felt in their spirit God said something to them or God wanted them to do something. And God does speak to people that way as he has to me also. But I mean hearing God speak to me personally and carrying on a conversation with him. The simplest way I can think to explain it to someone who has never had a conversation with God is this. As you read these words off of this paper to yourself, not out loud, you can hear yourself reading the words. That's the way God has sometimes chosen to speak to me. I can hear him in my mind, but not out loud, not an audible voice like when my wife talks to me. And he talks to me when I am not expecting it either.

Here is one example of a conversation I had with God. As long as I can remember I've been waiting to be old enough to drive. The automobile I had dreamed of owning the most was a Ford Mustang. We had saved up $3000 and I went to an all Ford car show in Canfield, Ohio. I spent the whole day looking at different cars but the only Mustang I could buy there was a six cylinder and that was not what I wanted. Six cylinders were for people who wanted to go slow and look good. I wanted eight cylinders for brute power and speed. Not long after that I was at home after work and the phone rang. My wife, Diana was calling me from her job in town. On her way to work that morning she had seen a Mustang for sale. She told me where it was and that after dinner we would go look at it. As soon as I hung up the phone I grabbed my car keys and out the door I went. I had just gotten out of my driveway headed for town when God asked. "Where are you going?"

I said, "You know where I am going, I am going to look at a Mustang."

God said, "That car is not for you."

And I said, "Yea Diana called me and told me about it so I'm going to look at it."

God said, "That car is not for you."

Then I started to plead my case, "Lord you know I have always wanted a Mustang. You know how I try to study the word every day, how I try to tell others about you as often as I can, how I pray every day. Does not your word say *Delight myself in the Lord and you will give me the desires of my heart.* Lord, haven't I done that? Please, I desire a Ford Mustang."

God said, "That car is not for you."

Now I am still making my way into town during this conversation with God. "Well," I said, "look, Lord, when I get there if it's under $6000, I'll know it's the one."

God said, "That car is not for you."

I said, "Lord, if it has under 70,000 miles I'll know it's the one."

God said, "That car is not for you."

Finally I said, "Lord if someone is home to let me look at the car and answer questions about it I'll know it's the one." What a loving and patient God we serve. God said, "That car is not for you."

When I got to the location where the car was, no one came to the door even though I beat on it for at least five minutes. It looked like the speedometer read 85,000 miles and the price on the for sale sign was $7200. I got back in my car and headed for home.

I said, "Well, Lord, I guess I'm not buying that Mustang."

God said, *"I told you that car is not for you."* Life is just that way sometimes God will tell us things or show us things that are not for us or good for us, but we keep trying to convince him we know better than he does, what's best for us. Instead of *your will be done* we think *my will be done.*

Diana got home from work and asked me if I wanted to go look at the Mustang. I told her I had run into town already. I had looked at the Mustang and said, "That is not the car for me."

Shortly thereafter Diana saw an ad in the newspaper for a 1989 Mustang GT at a car dealership for $8500. I said, "You know that's more than what we want to spend for a car right now."

Diana said, "Yes, but it has less than 50,000 miles. We can go look if you want."

If I want! I called to make sure they still had the car because the ad was in a paper that was almost two weeks old. They still had it so I got directions on how to get there. We were on the road in less than fifteen minutes. I took my car just in case we decided to buy, but I really wasn't too hopeful, not after the last time I went to look at a Mustang.

We arrived at the dealership and talked with a young salesman. He took us to see the car. It was beautiful. The salesman was a Mustang enthusiast. He started rattling off things about the car. I had no idea what most of it meant but he was excited about that Mustang. We took it for a test run and I just fell head over heels for that car. But I felt deep down that I would not be leaving with that car.

It was in perfect shape, no dents, bangs or scratches. My car, the one I brought to trade in, was a 1983 Ford Thunderbird with 98,000 miles. The tires needed to be replaced before the next inspection, the front brakes and rotors were shot and they needed replaced, plus I still owed money to the bank on it.

Well, someone took it for a test ride, came back and whispered something in the salesman's ear. He wrote some figures out on a piece of paper, then showed it to Diana and me. Just as I had suspected, they were not going to give us much for my car on trade-in, not even enough to pay it off at the bank. I told him, "Thanks, but the price is to much. We could not afford the Mustang at this time."

"Well" he said, "let me see what I can do for you. Wait right here," and he left the room. Now Diana knew how much I liked that car, you could see it in my face. Everybody there could tell, but I knew we just couldn't buy it on those terms.

The salesman came back with a different figure. With a smile on his face he asked, "How about this price?" The second price was better but still not what we thought we could afford. So we told him that was better but still not what we felt we could spend.

By this time I had already told the salesman how much I had always wanted a Mustang. He looked me square in the eyes and said, "You are not going home until I get you this car for a price you think you can afford." He left to go talk to somebody again. Diana and I went outside for some air and to talk. We decided as long as we could get the car for the same payment a month as the T-Bird we would buy it. I repeated to myself for about the tenth time a silent prayer, *Lord please let this be the one* but with no response from God.

We went back inside. The young salesman called us over to his desk and put a new figure in front of us. Diana and I looked down at the numbers, looked up at each other at the same time, and Diana must have seen a grin on my face from ear to ear. He had not only gotten the price down to what we were paying on the old T-Bird, he surpassed it. It was $20 a month cheaper!

"Thank you Jesus." I kept saying it over and over. I was in shock now. I could hardly believe it. We brought the car home and took it over to show Diana's mother and father. Her father said, "Bet that set you back a pretty penny."

I just smiled. I said, "My payments are cheaper than they were on that old T-Bird I had."

He said, "Oh, okay."

Chapter Four

*W*ith everything that I consider was going right in my life at that time, I was beginning to have frequent pains in my chest and an upset stomach quite often. I went to our family doctor finally and was diagnosed with a hiatal hernia, and acid reflux. The doctor gave me some pills to try and see if they helped. Now I have to confess some of the foods I ate were not helping my problem. I just like spicy foods, the hotter the better. I even made up a spicy hot ranch-flavored popcorn that I can't make enough of; my friends and co-workers just gobble it up. They just cannot seem to get enough of it. So I had to cut back on the spicy foods and take a pill every time I felt the heartburn coming on.

One afternoon after work I was sitting at home watching the *700 Club,* on Cornerstone, the inspirational channel I get on cable. This particular inspirational program, Monday through Friday, at the end of the program would have a couple of people pray for their TV audience. For example, they would have a word of knowledge about someone with a back problem and that it was being healed right then. All kinds of ailments they would pray for at the end of these TV programs. Then on different shows they would read testimonies that people sent in about how they had been healed from a sickness that was spoken about on TV. I remember thinking *I wish they would have a word of knowledge for me.* One that would clear up my hernia and heartburn problem. Every day I began to make sure I didn't miss the end of the show to see if they would call out my problem on TV.

You may be thinking why didn't you just ask God to heal you? I had, but for some reason God did not choose to heal me just by my asking him to. About the second week of waiting to hear about my condition, someone on the show had a word of knowledge for someone with a hiatal hernia caused from acid reflux. And they said, "If that's you just reach out your hand where you are right now. God is healing you."

I raised my hand toward the TV and said, "Lord that word was for me. I know it was." A warm tingling feeling started at the bottom of my chin in my throat area and worked its way down to just past my sternum. I just began to thank God for healing me. "Thank you, Jesus. Thank you, Jesus," I said it over and over, and I believed God healed me. I stopped taking the pills and had no problem with the heartburn or the hernia.

Romans 10-17 (KJV) *So then faith cometh by hearing, and hearing by the word of God.* I had watched this TV program enough and heard the testimonies from the people who would write in, that it help build my faith up. Then when I stepped out in faith God healed me. That just built up my faith even more. It gave me even more confidence in my walk with the Lord.

On that TV program they would use these verses from the Bible in Matthew 18:19-20, "Again, I tell you that if two of you on earth agree about anything you ask for, it will be done for you by my Father in heaven. For where two or three come together in my name, there am I with them." When the TV personality said there is someone who has a hiatal hernia caused from acid reflux. We agreed on that it was the problem I had and together we also agreed that God could fix my problem. God's word is true.

One Sunday someone at our church spoke on fasting and praying. He told how it helps him grow closer to the Lord. I thought I was doing pretty good with my walk, but this person was very convincing. So I looked up some verses on fasting. After studying and praying about it I decided to give it a try.

Now in the Bible there are several different time tables for fasting. There is the one day fast, two days, three days, seven days, fourteen days, twenty-one days, and forty days. And then there is the modern day one meal fast. I liked that one the best cause I like to eat. So I humbled myself and told Diana no lunch for me, I'm fasting on Wednesdays from now on instead of eating. At lunch I'm going to pray. "Ok," she said, "but count me out. I have to eat or I will get a headache."

"That's all right," I said, sort of with a prideful attitude.

The following Wednesday was one of the longest days of my entire life, or so it seemed. I drank about three cans of pop, drank a bottle of orange juice, and about a gallon of water. And have you ever tried to pray for thirty minutes? I prayed and prayed and prayed, then I looked at the clock. Ten minutes! Something must be wrong with that clock. But it wasn't I just never had sat down and tried to pray for thirty minutes before. I would pray at different times during the day but not long prayers.

As soon as I got home after work I was eating everything in sight. But I was faithful I keep it up. Every Wednesday I had no food at work. And my prayer time got better as time went by. After a while I even stopped eating everything as soon as I got home I made it until dinner. There are many reasons or answers people give for fasting. This is mine. When I am fasting and praying I am showing my heavenly Father that the spiritual part of me is in control of the physical part of me, at least for a short period of time if it's only for one meal. But as you take control of your physical self you find out you can fast if you rely on God's strength to help you. Philippians 4:13 (KJV) *I can do all things through Christ which strengtheneth me.* When you take your mind off of food, concentrate on Christ and your relationship with him. He will more than give you the strength to accomplish the fast you have set before yourself.

Our children were growing up so fast, our lives were so busy. We liked to go camping, we liked boating and fishing. I had also become a racing nut. On every other Saturday night I raced a riding mower on a circle 1/8 mile dirt track. What a blast! It was not only a family affair but also my neighbors had gotten involved in it too. My one neighbor, Chuck, was my pit man; he helped with getting the mowers ready to race. And my other neighbor, Keith, would watch me on my hot laps and give me advice on adjustments I might need to make to my racing mower. And their wives, Brenda and Helen, would come and give their support also. My in-laws, Joe, Beva, Dave and Beth would also come and watch me race. My mother-in-law told me later that she prayed extra hard that I would not get hurt.

Now I know you must be thinking *lawn mower racing, how dangerous could that be.* Well, my slightly modified stock eight hp riding mower would go about forty-three miles per hour. That's pretty quick on an oval banked dirt track with nothing but a neck brace and a helmet for safety equipment. I didn't wreck too many times but one evening I rolled my mower with my automobile keys in my pants pocket and I bent my trunk key with my leg. Now that hurt. Never again did I race with keys in my pocket.

By my third racing season I won the eight hp stock class points championship. While all these other things were going on in our lives, I had slacked off of my Bible studies and let other things take up time in my life. Not that they are bad, they just took my time away from my studies.

When I was thirty-seven, our church was having a hard time with getting people to come to church, especially the younger adults like us with children. They had become almost nonexistent, along with the children of the church. It seemed every week it became a battle to get our children ready for church. They would say, "We don't want to go, it's not fun anymore, and there is nobody else in our Sunday school class." You get the picture. But my wife Diana grew up in that Baptist church. She had been going there almost her entire life plus we had not only met there but were also married there. And I had gotten a lot of support from our pastor with my studies and the opportunity for me to preach there. But we had some convincing statements from other young couples who had already left and found a new church, a church with lots of children. We decided that for the betterment of our children and family altogether we would give this new church a try.

The first Sunday was almost a culture shock. It was a nondenominational contemporary church. There were no pews to sit in. Cushioned chairs lined the sanctuary, if you would call it that, more like a small auditorium. Stage up front, multicolored lights hanging from the ceiling like they have at concerts, microphones, a set of drums, a couple of guitars and a baby grand piano. No stained glass windows or steeple on top of the building. There was a welcome center with coffee and several other kinds of drinks with donuts or cookies. Not only that, you could take them inside the sanctuary if you wanted to.

When the music started the words were projected up on the wall at the back of the stage. And it wasn't the songs we were used to, those old spiritual hymns. No these were upbeat songs, new contemporary Christian music. Feet stomping, hand clapping, jump up and down spiritual songs. The Bible says, in Psalm 98:4 (KJV) *Make a joyful noise unto the Lord, all the earth: make a loud noise, and rejoice, and sing praise.* And let me tell you they did. They had a time for shaking hands and welcoming everyone to the service.

Then the preacher got up to give his message but he didn't look like a preacher. He had on a multi-colored shirt and a pair of shorts. He didn't stand behind a pulpit and talk in that preacher voice they learn at seminary. He just read from the Bible and talked like he would if he were sitting at a table having a cup of coffee, shooting the breeze with you. He got the point across and that was it. Our children liked the new church. Why wouldn't they, there were children everywhere we looked. Diana and I just felt that at this time in our lives it would be better to move to this new church so the children would want to go. And they had a great youth program for the children too.

So we said goodbye to friends and family at the Baptist church. We began attending the new contemporary nondenominational church. Diana's mother was sad at our decision to leave the church but agreed it would be better for the children. I always like to consider Diana's mother's thoughts on things because I considered her to be a wise spiritual mother.

We started worshiping at our new church and we seemed to fit in pretty well. Not long after we had been going there they had a church picnic. We played tennis, softball, basketball, volleyball. We threw frisbees, the children played on the playground, in the sand box, you name it. I think we pretty much covered it all that day. There was a huge spread of food, everything you could imagine was on the food table. Then afterwards it was karaoke time. We sat around in lawn chairs and listened as different people got up to sing. Children, adults, young and old alike were having a ball singing their hearts out. Some were good, some not so good. Some made us laugh, some made us cry. I even got up the courage to sing in front of all of those new friends we had made.

All in all it was a great day. We got to know many of the church members that day on a little more personal level. And after they found out that I could sing they asked if Diana sang also. When we told them she could they ask Diana and me if we would join the praise team that lead the singing on Sunday mornings. But we didn't want to just jump in right away so we told them not now, but later on we would. We wanted to get more acquainted with some of the new songs before getting up in front of the church.

We were very pleased with our new church home. There was no pressure on me to get a Sunday school lesson ready every week, no church board meeting to attend, no one telling me how the church should be doing this or doing that. No more filling in for the pastor. It was like we were on vacation. I loved it.

But there were struggles and trials that not only I, but my family began to face also. Diana had become restless. She just could not sleep through a whole night. So a co-worker suggested we have a hot toddy before bed. He knew how much I liked spicy foods so he suggested a couple of shots of a hot cinnamon drink before bedtime. So I stopped by the liquor store and picked up a bottle to try it out. Diana wasn't too keen on the idea. She hadn't drunk alcoholic beverages before other than a little champagne at weddings. So I told her, "Look, Jesus drank wine. We are just gonna have a couple of shots. We'll see if it helps you sleep at night. If it doesn't you don't have to drink it any more." We had our couple of shots before bedtime and she slept like a baby that night. So every night after that we would have our hot toddy before bed.

The winter months had become quite a challenge for us driving in them. Diana wrecked the Mustang one winter and the next winter I wrecked my truck. We got rid of the Mustang bought a Ford Taurus, but Diana slid on black ice and totaled that car. So we parked my truck and bought me a winter beater. We bought Diana another Ford Taurus. But because the accidents were all within a twelve month period, we were put on high risk by our insurance company, and our auto insurance jumped to a little over $3000 a year. So we decided to sell our newer automobiles that were financed and buy older ones we could pay cash for. That way we could insure them with liability only but that was still going to be about $1500 a year.

Our middle son was having some issues of his own. He did not like going to church so when we moved to the new church we did not make him go. He was having a lot of difficulties at school. Seemed like he had detention every other week. He was missing school a lot. He would stay up late, then not want to get up for school. Diana and I dealt with those things fairly well, I thought. But when school was out that year he left home one weekend and did not return. He did call us a few days later that next week, but told us he would not be coming home soon. He said he just needed to work some things out for himself.

That was a tough summer for Diana and myself. We did not know where he was, what he was doing, if he was eating. He was on our minds a lot. We said many prayers for his safe return. Finally after a little over two months he was picked up by the police as a runaway and we had to go pick him up.

When we first saw him after what seemed to be the longest summer of our lives, I felt like the father in the parable Jesus taught in Luke 15:11-24, "There was a man who had two sons. The younger

one said to his father, 'Father, give me my share of the estate.' So he divided his property between them. Not long after that, the younger son got together all he had, set off for a distant country and there squandered his wealth in wild living. After he had spent everything, there was a severe famine in that whole country, and he began to be in need. So he went and hired himself out to a citizen of that country, who sent him to his fields to feed pigs. He longed to fill his stomach with the pods that the pigs were eating, but no one gave him anything. When he came to his senses, he said, 'How many of my father's hired men have food to spare, and here I am starving to death! I will set out and go back to my father and say to him: Father, I have sinned against heaven and against you. I am no longer worthy to be called your son; make me like one of your hired men.' So he got up and went to his father. But while he was still a long way off, his father saw him and was filled with compassion for him; he ran to his son, threw his arms around him and kissed him. The son said to him, 'Father; I have sinned against heaven and against you. I am no longer worthy to be called your son.' But the father said to his servants, 'Quick! Bring the best robe and put it on him. Put a ring on his finger and sandals on his feet. Bring the fattened calf and kill it. Let's have a feast and celebrate. For this son of mine was dead and is alive again; he was lost and is found.' So they began to celebrate."
I was very glad to see our son. Inside I was relieved and happy, I gave him a hug and a kiss, Diana too. But unlike the father in the parable, I also felt like kicking his behind for all he had put Diana and myself through that summer, but I didn't. We had some issues that we had to work out together and some issues he had to work out on his own. All in all everything turned out ok.

That summer after Diana would go to bed at night I would stay up and watch TV. That wasn't unusual. I had almost always done that, I was a night owl. What I was doing different was after we had our little

~ 56 ~

hot toddy I would tuck Diana in bed, go back downstairs wait ten or fifteen minutes and go into the kitchen and have another couple of shots, sit down, relax and watch TV. After a couple of weeks or so though I would add another shot. After a while I didn't want to do anything but go to work, come home, cook supper, get the children off to their bedrooms by 8:30 or 9:00 p.m. and start drinking. Instead of seeking out the peace of God, I began to try then to find peace of mind and relaxation from everyday life from the bottle.

After we had moved to the new church we eventually joined the worship team but we only had to help once sometimes twice a month, that was it. This was a time of great fellowship with the other singers on the worship team, Diana and I learned a lot of new contemporary Christian songs but there was no Sunday school class to study for. They did have small groups that met together but we just didn't seem to find the time to get plugged into one of those groups. I had slipped into a laziness mode, no studying of the Bible on my own. All the word I got was from the preacher on Sunday morning. I had stopped fasting. I had stopped chewing tobacco a few years earlier but picked up the habit again. That summer was particularly hot so I decided to cut off my long hair. I was starving for spiritual food, but instead of feeding my spirit like I should have, I let my fleshly body, my sinful nature, take control over my spirit again. I was again feeding my fleshly body more and more and more. I no longer cared as much about the spiritual things in my life as I did the fleshly things.

That's why it is so important to read God's word, the Holy Bible, everyday. That's why we need to stay in tuned to the Holy Spirit. We start doing things in the flesh we know we shouldn't do. The Holy Spirit speaks to us, tell us "No" and what do we do? We ignore him and after a while we don't hear him anymore. So we take on life on our own.

There were two different occasions during this time in my life, that could have cost me my life if God had not had mercy on me. "Wake up calls," if you will, that I didn't pay any attention to. I was at the dentist office getting a tooth pulled. The night before I had been drinking as usual. The next day I sat in the dentist chair, scared to death. One of my greatest fears was the dentist. I know to some people that seems silly, but not to me. I had been going to the dentist so often in those years trying to get my teeth fixed from all the damage I had done to them from chewing tobacco and just not taking care of them. I was horrified every time I sat in the dentist chair. That particular day after I had the tooth pulled the dentist had left the room, and the assistant was with me. The assistant gave me a drink to rinse out my mouth with. I put the rinse in my mouth the assistant left the room to go see another patient. As she left me alone my mouth was still half numb. That mixed with the alcohol still in my system, that they knew nothing about, and my fear got me so worked up I passed out, then choked with my mouth full of the rinse.

The next thing I knew the dentist and the assistant were sitting over me bringing me back to consciousness. As I came to, the dentist told the assistant to go call 911 and cancel the ambulance call. I had been out long enough and had the dentist worried enough to call 911. She made me stay there long enough to make sure I was okay to drive home.

A few short months later I had another tooth pulled. This time I made it home ok but I decided that the pain pills the dentist gave me were not strong enough for the pain I was in so I decided to mix alcohol with the pills. At first it was fine; I felt no pain at all. But after a while I went from feeling no pain to feeling sweat break out and hives breaking out on my body. My chest began to hurt and then fear attacked me. I told Diana I was sick, that she needed to take me to the emergency room. We got in the car and on the way there I just knew I was a goner.

We arrived at the hospital. They checked me in and immediately began working on me. By this time my throat was beginning to swell shut. After telling the doctors what I had been drinking and what kind of pain pill I had taken they figured out how to help me. I spent several hours in the emergency room for making dumb choices during that time of my life.

At times we can be stubborn people. The Bible tells us in Ephesians 4:30, "And do not grieve the Holy Spirit of God." When we stop listening to the Holy Spirit's advice we can get into a world of trouble. While all this is going on we think in our minds we have everything under control but of course we don't. Self is in control but not under control. Whenever we let self be in control and not God we lose every time.

I can remember a few years ago thinking about the Israelites when Moses brought them out of Egypt. They continually made the same mistakes over and over. They would mess up ask Moses to talk to God. God would fix the problem and then the Israelites would mess up again. They would go to Moses again to talk to God on their behalf and God would fix the problem again. And I thought to myself those were some stubborn and dumb people. They were continually being disobedient to God. What was their problem, were they thick headed or what? But now, looking back, I can see the same pattern throughout my life. It's so easy for us to point the finger at someone else, when we need to be looking in a mirror at our own lives.

By the time I was forty-one we had been going to the new church for about four years. The original pastor and his family had moved on to start another church. By this time the church was on its third pastor. People were coming and some were going, like a lot of churches these days it seems. But there was that faithful group of people that was there week after week. This was not a handful of people; this was around 125 to 150 on an average week. Diana and I were still singing on the praise team. And even though I wasn't living the Christian life that I could or should have been, God used that time to prepare us for future work in store for us. I was however, beginning to have some health problems about this time. Sometimes when I swallowed my food it would get stuck three-quarters of the way down my throat. The first few times this happened it nearly scared me to death. I thought I was going to chock to death. Once at work I was eating an apple and a piece of it got stuck in my throat. So I stepped outside the door in my work area to get a drink of pop. The pop was outside because it was winter and we would buy pop to share, keep it outdoors to stay cold. One of my co-workers at that time, Dave, locked me outside. Now he didn't know I was choking, but at the time that didn't matter. I was outside freaking out, beating on the door and choking. But I calmed down and the food slid down my throat. I got a drink of pop walked around to another door to get back inside. I told Dave that I was outside choking thanks a lot. He didn't know I was choking, he apologized and that was that. Dave, who doesn't work beside me any longer, every now and then will ask me, "Do you want a piece of apple?" We both laugh and I tell him "No thank you."

But this became an ongoing thing. I began eating a lot of mashed potatoes and gravy, creamed soups, anything soft. Now I had come to the conclusion that my bad teeth were the problem. Chewing tobacco all those years was hard on my teeth. I had been going to the dentist for the last five years continually having them worked on but they kept getting worse and worse. So I decided to have them all pulled out and get dentures. Pretty sad if you think about it here I was in my early forties and I needed to get dentures. Not because

I was in an accident or something that I couldn't have avoided, but pure negligence on my part, not taking proper care of my teeth. So I had them all pulled and got my new dentures. My mouth was sore for a while so I had to eat soft food. But after a while I tried eating solid food again but the same thing happened. I was still choking on solid food so I just gave up.

The dentures made me gag so I took them out. Without my teeth when I would sing I sounded funny. I could not sound out some of the words in the songs we sang at church so I dropped out of the worship team. Also because of drinking 140 proof liquor every night, I began having stomach problems and vomiting on an average of every other night. It was a horrible feeling to be awakened from a deep sleep to be choking and trying to run for the bathroom to vomit. I am so ashamed now that I let myself slip back into sin like that.

Because of living in my sinful nature at that time in my life, I lost something I had received from God. I no longer had my miracle healing. One of the most important things God ever did for me to help build my faith I destroyed by returning to living a sinful life style. Oh, I still looked good in the day but at night I was not the same. Sin was controlling me, not the Holy Spirit. In the gospel of John 5:8-14 (KJV) *Jesus said unto him, Rise take up thy bed and walk. And immediately the man was made whole, and took up his bed, and walked: and on the same day was the sabbath. The Jews therefore said unto him that was cured, It is the sabbath day; it is not lawful for thee to carry thy bed. He answered them, He that made me whole, the same said unto me, Take up thy bed, and walk. Then asked they him, What man is that which said unto thee, Take up thy bed and walk? And he that was healed wist not who it was; for Jesus had conveyed himself away, a multitude being in that place. Afterward Jesus findeth him in the temple, and said unto him, Behold, thou art made whole: sin no more, lest a worse thing come unto thee.* You see Jesus had healed this man who had been a cripple but now could walk but Jesus gave him a warning to "Sin No More." I had been living an upright and victorious Christian life in Jesus when I was healed of my acid reflux and hiatal hernia. But I chose to return to my old ways once again, back to my old sinful ways of living, serving God outwardly only and not internally from my heart. God wants our hearts to be right toward him, not just how we act. Our whole being, inside and out both of them. That 140 proof liquor was not good for my stomach but I didn't care. I kept right on drinking it night after night. There is no doubt if I had not started drinking alcohol and chewing tobacco again, I would still be cured from that particular health problem.

Someone may say, "Well, it really wasn't a miracle cure if you got sick again."

But I say, "Yes it was." I trusted God to heal me and he did, but God also trusted me to Sin No More. And for a period of time I didn't. But I let down my guard and slipped back into that sin, not just any sin, because we all sin, but a sin that I had left behind, sin that through the help of the Holy Spirit I had overcome. The sin of destroying God's temple, my body, by drinking alcohol excessively and chewing tobacco.

Oh the trails we travel on in this life. The choices we make should not be done lightly. In Philippians 4:6-7, "Do not be anxious about anything, but in everything, by prayer and petition, with thanksgiving, present your request to God. And the peace of God, which transcends all understanding, will guard your hearts and your minds in Christ Jesus."

We need to make it our prayer every day that the choices we are making at that particular time in our lives are the right choices for our lives. If I had been praying about the things that were going on in my life at that time, asking God to give me wisdom in some of my choices, the Holy Spirit would have helped me make better choices. I know that he would have simple as that.

By this time not only had my spiritual life backslid, my health was deteriorating. Over a period of about ten months I lost about forty-five pounds. I had gotten to the point that I would only eat mashed potatoes and eat creamed soups. Every time I tried to eat solid food it would get stuck in my throat. So I would put food in my mouth chew on it for a while then spit it out so I did not choke on it. Finally my family doctor said that I needed to go see a throat specialist. The specialist wanted to take an X-ray of me swallowing some thick chalky stuff with a chunk of cookie in it. After that ordeal the doctor wanted to run a scope down my throat to check it out.

The day came to have the test done at the hospital. I was so nervous. I had not been put to sleep in a hospital since I was five and had my tonsils taken out. But the doctor assured me she did this a lot and everything would be ok. After the procedure was over we found out that my throat looked like an hour glass. All of the vomiting I had been doing had ruined a section of my throat. It had basically collapsed at one point and that's where the food was getting stuck. But while the doctor was in there with the scope she ballooned my throat and fixed it. "Now I should be ok," she said. But I also have Barrett's disease and she needed to check on that periodically. I now had a greater chance of getting throat cancer because of having this disease. I could now swallow and eat real food again.

It did not take long, a few short months to put that weight back on. One year later I had my throat scoped again and everything was okay. I did not have to have it done again for three years unless I began having problems swallowing again.

All through this time of my life I was still drinking but by now I had become a drunkard. Now I had gone from a couple shots a night to half a fifth a night. I could not go to sleep like a normal person. I had to drink myself to sleep. I tried to quit drinking but I stayed up almost all night and then I was too tired to go to work. So I would give up and just start drinking again. But at one point late at night (actually it was early in the morning, between 1:00 and 2:00 a.m.) I went upstairs and told my wife, "I need help." I could not stop drinking by myself and I wanted her to call her mother and tell her to pray for me. Diana told me to call her myself.

So as drunk as I was, I went back downstairs and called my mother-in-law. She answered the phone and we talked. She agreed not only to pray for me but to make sure I would seek out the help I needed. That was a very hard thing for me to do, to call my mother-in-law for she was a very devoted Christian woman. She was not only my mother-in-law, but she had been in my Sunday school class when I taught at the Baptist Church we had left. She was there every time I had preached before we left the Baptist Church. She knew all about my spiritual life, but had never gotten a glimpse of my sinful life.

She was shocked to find out the life of a drunk I lived at night, but oh, so willing to pray for me to help me in any way she could and to encourage me not to continue in it any longer. I went to our family doctor and asked to be put in an alcohol rehab. He asked me, "Do you really want to stop drinking?"

I told him, "Yes, I really do. I have tried and tried but I just can't do it by myself. Every time I try to stop drinking I cannot sleep, so I go back to drinking so I can sleep."

So we decided to try sleeping pills first and see if that would work instead of rehab. I took the pills for two weeks and after my body got trained to fall asleep at night like I should, then I stopped taking them. After my ordeal was over my mother-in-law never brought it up again and never told anyone else in our family about it.

Chapter Five

*W*hen I was forty-two, Diana and I stopped our regular church attendance and only went every now and then. So after a while we just stopped going altogether. Diana and I both liked the outdoors so much, in fact, that spring through fall we would go fishing on Sundays instead of going to church. We have owned many watercrafts since we have been married, and have spent many a day and night on the water not only fishing, but boating in general. We have owned canoes, paddle boats, speed boats, fishing boats, and a pontoon boat.

Diana's mother knew we had stopped going to church. She would call and ask us Sunday evening if we had gone to church. We would tell her no, we had spent the day on the lake instead. She would nicely get on our case and ask us to come back to her church but we declined. "Well," she'd say, "you need to go to church somewhere," and she was right, but we just wanted to handle life own our own for a while.

Or so we thought. We just didn't want to go to church anywhere at that time in our lives. We did go with her and my father-in-law on the holidays and that seemed to suffice with her for a while. But she never gave up on us. From time to time she would still ask if we were going to church.

Now of course we thought we were having the time of our lives, but in reality we weren't. We just didn't know it at that time. We worked all week long and on the weekends we did whatever we wanted to do. Camping, boating, fishing, shopping, going out to eat, we did it all. Since we were not going to church we had this extra money we used to give to the church. We lived high on the hog so to speak. But it didn't take long until that extra money just kind of disappeared. Then before we knew it Diana was struggling to pay the bills every month. But we hung in there and made it somehow month to month.

Now at this junction in our lives I had sold a nice trihull boat that we owned before winter to help catch up our bills. The next spring I bought a small 12 ft. aluminum boat from one of my co-workers. It was perfect for using on the river. We also used it on the lake away from the big boats.

Now this particular day was the Forth of July. We had gotten up early, loaded up the boat with a cooler of food, drinks for us, and plenty of bait for the fish. It was a beautiful morning and we had been catching some fish here and there but mostly small ones we threw back. Diana noticed off in the distance that the sky had turned from a pretty blue to a couple of dark clouds here and there, I told her not to worry about it, the clouds would blow over. And sure enough they did. Now with the slight weather change all of a sudden we were beginning to catch fish on a more regular basis with larger fish being landed in the boat.

Then the clouds turned dark once more, Diana began to point out the weather to me again. After checking out the sky, I assured her that it would blow over once again. We were now catching fish quite frequently and I was having a ball. But Diana, on the other hand, was starting to become a little annoyed at the situation. We were a good thirty-to-forty minute boat ride back to our truck and the loading dock. And I just kept ignoring the sky and kept right on catching fish.

Finally Diana put her fishing pole away and just sat there. I said, "Are you done?"

She told me, "Yes I am done and you need to be done to. Look at the sky. It is black now on the other end of the lake. If we left right now we would be lucky to get back to the dock before the storm hits."

I looked straight at her and said, "I am not leaving yet. Look at all the fish I am catching, and nice ones too. The Lord could take me right now and I would be just fine with that." I had barely gotten those words out of my mouth when a lightning bolt struck toward the upper end of the lake.

There are no words to describe what I felt at that moment but needless to say I had a change of heart. I wasn't ready for the Lord to take me at that moment. I changed my mind. I started up the boat motor and away we went. We had not gotten ten minutes into our ride back to the dock when the rain hit and the thunder and lightning moved in right on top of us. So I just headed straight for the shore line to get out of that metal boat we were in. I figured I like my chances on the land instead of on the water.

I had that little boat motor wide open running it as hard as it would go. About forty-yards from the shore line the boat came to a sudden stop. Thump! And the motor stopped running. We had hit an underwater stump. I tried to pull the rope to restart the motor, but it would not move. I put the trolling motor down into the water just enough to move the boat along so I didn't hit another stump and finally made it to the shore.

The wind was blowing like mad, it was still pouring down rain with thunder and lighting, and now we had to walk through the woods to get to the road so we could find a house for help. And as if that was not bad enough Diana wasn't too happy with me, either. Soaking wet, we made it through the woods and not too far up the road was a house. Luckily, there was someone home. As Diana and I stood there soaking wet I looked into a window in the door. I could see a number of people inside eating their Forth of July meal. Someone came to the door and I explained to him how we had been fishing, were caught on the lake in the storm and needed a ride to our truck. He asked us to wait there and went back inside for a minute, returned and said okay. I apologized for interrupting his meal. He said that was okay and gave us a ride to the boat dock where we pick up our truck and boat trailer and went home.

Assessing our dilemma, we came up with a plan to get our boat home. It took two trips to the lake in between rain storms and the rest of the day to finally get the boat home. The second trip the battery was just about dead and it was getting late when someone in a speed boat came by. He towed me in the last half of a mile. I thanked the boater for the tow then loaded our boat and went home. As I sat at home that night and reflected on the day gone by I realized what a fool I had been. God had given us a beautiful morning on the lake we had caught some nice fish. But I had become greedy and arrogant. I had refused good counsel from my wife. I had not only put our lives in harm's way but had damaged the motor so badly it could not be fixed.

Psalm 107:17 says, "Some became fools through their rebellious ways and suffered affliction because of their iniquities." I was living a rebellious life style and was now suffering for it. Not only had I lived out this terrible day on the lake, I kept begging God to help me get the boat to the dock. I was terrified, and rightly so. I hadn't asked God for forgiveness, just to please; please get me and the boat back safely. I was more interested in that boat than my relationship with God. How arrogant I must have sounded to God when I said he could just take me now. I certainly didn't fear God when I spoke those words out of my mouth. Proverbs 1:7 says, "The fear of the Lord is the beginning of knowledge, but fools despise wisdom and discipline." That day God had gotten my attention, but I was not done rebelling yet.

One of the couples we had met at the contemporary church were outdoor people too. They like fishing, camping and also motorcycling. I hadn't owned a motorcycle since my teenage years and the death of my friend Terry. But Diana and I talked it over and we decided to buy a used motorcycle to see if we would like doing that on the weekends. I could also ride it to work to save on gas. We looked and looked until December, when I finally found one I liked at a decent price. I had a buddy from work try it out for me, since I did not have a motorcycle license yet. He gave me his approval and so we bought it. We purchased a couple of helmets and I rode the motorcycle that winter on nice days. The next spring we rode the motorcycle over to Diana's mother and father's house to show them. Diana's father was a little shocked, but Diana's mother just told us to be safe and to have fun on it.

It was a Kawasaki Ltd 440 and it was a lot of fun. That summer we would meet up with our friends from the contemporary church on Sunday mornings along with a number of other riders they knew and go for rides. They had stopped attending church on Sundays too. We would go on all-day rides and have a lot of fun, usually stopping somewhere on the ride during the day for a good meal.

Several days I rode the motorcycle to work. In the morning during the fall it would be cold, but in the afternoon on the ride home it was a nice ride. I always left early in the morning because of all the deer here in western Pennsylvania, and I drove fairly slow. On the rides home, though, I would ride at a little quicker pace.

One particular afternoon on my ride home, out of the blue a deer ran right in front of me. I hit the brakes hard and slid about ten yards before knocking the feet out from under the deer. I got the motorcycle stopped and the deer ran off unhurt. After I gathered myself together, and said a couple of "Thank you Lords," I headed for home. But the motorcycle had a knocking sound coming from the back wheel. I stopped checked it over but could find nothing wrong with it so I drove it home very slowly. I took it to the motorcycle shop and found out I had popped a rivet out of the sprocket and hub of the back wheel. They said it could not be pop-riveted back together without the risk of breaking the back wheel since it was so old. A new rim and the labor was going to be more than I could spend so I thanked them, took it home, and put a nut and bolt in it instead. The motorcycle stopped making the noise and it cost me nothing but a nut and bolt I already had. Needless to say I didn't ride the motorcycle to work anymore that year.

After what seemed to be a long winter spring finally came. We could hardly wait until we began our motorcycle rides on Sundays again. That summer the group we rode with on Sundays got bigger and bigger. We were having a tough time keeping up with them on the rides, or so it seemed to us. No one was leaving us behind; I was in reality just ready to look like the rest of our group that had newer bikes. Our bike was over twenty years old and everyone else's (I believed) were five years or newer. So in July we went to a couple of bike shops and picked out two motorcycles we liked. Put in loan applications and waited for the outcome. The cheaper of the two called first and we had been turned down for the loan. Naturally I wasn't very happy about it, but the other bike shop was bigger and had more financing options. They called about an hour later and would finance the motorcycle if we came up with a big down payment. I convinced Diana to clean out what little money we had in our savings account so we could buy it. I would then sell the old motorcycle to retrieve some of the money. We picked up the new motorcycle, which made me very happy.

We rode it with our friends on Sundays for about five weeks. But then I noticed oil leaking out of it onto the floor of the garage. I took the bike to the shop and they kept it for six weeks. I was so upset I wanted to trade it in on a new one, but they would only give me half of what I paid for it and it was only two months old. Finally we got it back but by then the Sunday rides were over.

I have always liked to watch movies as long as I can remember. I had at one time over 500 movies on videos. During the winter months especially I would watch movies. Action movies were my favorite. Fast cars, fast bikes, and fast boats made the action movie even better. And I can watch the same movie if I like it several times, that's why I liked buying the movie videos.

That winter one of the movies I watched was about fast cars. The whole movie was fast paced and the cars were not mega V8 motor cars, but mostly high tech four cylinder cars. I was so obsessed with this movie that I watched it thirty-six days in a row. I had a lot of the actors lines in the movie memorized. Diana used to shake her head at me for saying the lines while I watched the movie. The only reason I stopped watching it, I got sick and spent a whole day in bed mostly sleeping. But after that I would still watch it from time to time.

The following spring I found a nice used little sporty four cylinder car a ZX2 I just had to have it so I bought it. I drove it to work only a couple of times to show my friends at work, but I drove it mostly on the weekend. I had a fun time driving that little car around on the weekends. But after a while the novelty wore off.

Things of this world, worldly things, as the Bible says, that we own do not bring us joy. I don't know who I thought I was having a weekend car. It was just another payment I had put on my wife to try and pay each month. I had a void in my life but I was so blinded by everything I was doing I did not realize it.

Romans 1:28 says, "Furthermore, since they did not think it worthwhile to retain the knowledge of God, he gave them over to a depraved mind, to do what ought not to be done." My mind had become void of the things of God. I did not care about the things of God any longer, or so I thought. God was still there but I just did not have time for him. It was like I had packed God in a box and stored him away in the closet. I just kept trying to put other things in God's place but they were not filling the emptiness I had deep down inside.

About five months later my work truck broke down so I decided to trade in the ZX2 for another work truck and sell my old truck because it was no longer dependable. With all of this going on in my life, even though I was not faithful to God, on occasion God still showed his favor toward me. Diana and I went looking for another work truck. We were looking for a three or four year old truck with no more than 50,000 miles on it. We had picked one out that we liked at a local automobile lot. The salesman was going back and forth to the manager like they do trying to get the sale, when all of a sudden my wife said to me, "Look at this new truck here in the showroom. Wouldn't you like to have this one?"

Of course I said, "Yes I would." It was bright yellow. I thought that was the best looking truck I had ever seen in my life. But I knew that we could not afford a new truck.

The salesman came back and saw us looking at the new truck. He could obviously tell how much I liked it and said, "Would you rather buy that new truck instead of the used one?"

I just laugh at him and said, "Yeah right."

But the salesman said, "You know the payment on the new truck will be about the same as the payment on the used truck and you will have a warranty on the new truck, whereas on the used one you will have to buy a warranty."

I could not believe it. *Was this for real?* I thought to myself. The salesman checked on the payment on the new truck and sure enough with a little bargaining we left that day with that brand new bright yellow truck. Many times throughout my life God has shown me favor when I certainly did not deserve it. And that was just one of those times.

It was about this time in my life I had another dream I believe was from God. This dream was not like the other two I had before at all. This time the dream was like a cartoon; it was animated. I was fishing by myself when all of a sudden I got a bite on the end of my fishing line. Getting excited, I set the hook and began reeling in my catch. It was a monster of a fish and I was having a hard time getting the fish to shore, when all of a sudden fighting with the fish I pulled hard and snapped my fishing line about 10 feet out. I could see the ripple in the water where the line snapped and the fish got away. I threw down the fishing pole and dove into the water where the ripple started from. As I passed through the water level on the surface, underneath I landed on a dry surface breathing normally, instead of like someone who would be blowing bubbles swimming under water.

I looked around and saw a lot of fish in a pile just kind of flopping around. As I walked over toward the big pile of fish I was looking for the one with a hook and line still in its mouth. I began working my way around the pile of fish when I spotted the one I was looking for. It was the biggest fish in the pile. I walked over grabbed it with all my might and walked out of the lake grinning from ear to ear. I had such a hold on that big fish I knew it was not going to get away.

At the time of my dream I did not think much about it. I thought it was just a regular dream. Not like the dreams from God I had earlier in my life. There was no guess work about them. They were straight and to the point, but not this one. It was different. This dream I not only remembered when I awoke, but I could not get it out of my mind.

I told my wife the dream. I went to work and told my co-workers about the dream. Most of them thought it was a cool dream, but that was about it. And for weeks that dream would just pop into my head for no apparent reason.

Fast forwarding months later I was reading in Daniel chapter 2, about a dream King Nebuchadnezzar had that troubled him. He called together magicians, astrologers, sorcerers, and the Chaldeans to tell them his dream and get their interpretation of it. But they told the king that his request was too great. That no one could do such a thing. So the king said to them that if they could not do it all the wise men in Babylon would die. Daniel found out about the decree and asked the king for a little time and he would tell him what he wanted to know. Daniel asked his three friends to pray with him that God would have mercy on them and show Daniel the secret dream and the interpretation of it. God did have mercy on them and showed Daniel the dream and the interpretation of the king's dream. And so all the wise men's lives were spared, including Daniel and his three friends.

As I read this story from the Bible I remembered my fishing dream. In Daniel 2:28 (KJV) *But there is a God in heaven that revealth secrets.* So I asked God to reveal to me the interpretation of the fishing dream I kept remembering if it was important. And the revelation of the dream I received was this: During the time of my dream I was living a life style that was not consistent to a Christian life. My dream was God's way of once again trying to get my attention, even though at the time I didn't realize it. The big fish I was struggling with on my line and had lost was Jesus. That even the line had been broken between us, which was our relationship, by my fighting against him, and not doing things I knew I should be doing as a Christian. I needed to jump back into my relationship with Jesus. Grab a hold of him as hard as I could and not let go. Because of all the fish in this world to catch there is none bigger than Jesus Christ, the son of God. It just goes to show us that even though we might walk away from our relationship with Jesus, sometimes God tries to get our attention in many different ways hoping to draw us back into his fellowship.

Chapter Six

When I was forty-five we made a trip down home to Mississippi to visit my family. We stayed with my mother at her home and visited with my siblings and their families. My mother had not been feeling well for some time. After a dinner we all had together our mother sat down with all her children and told us what was wrong with her. She had found out that she had throat cancer. Of course we were all in shock. She explained all she could to us about her cancer and what she had decided to do as far as treatments. My oldest sister had just the week before had her gall bladder taken out. Then I found out that one of my other sisters was separated from her husband, getting a divorce and struggling financially trying to raise her two children. It was supposed to be a week-long vacation visiting with my family and having fun. But the fun time of our vacation was overturned with nothing but bad news after bad news. It depressed me so much that after only three days I decided I had all of vacation I could handle, packed up and headed back to Pennsylvania.

I called my mother on the phone more often now because eventually she was to lose her voice. Then I would never hear her voice again. I was so hit by this news of my mother that even though I was still praying to God every day he seemed to be farther and farther away. And of course I did not help matters either by my actions.

About this time in my life I decided to pick up the bottle once more. Earlier in the summer I had tried an apple flavored alcoholic beverage that I had become very fond of. I would only have one at suppertime with my dinner and another one sometime before bedtime. But as time went by and I seemed to become a little more depressed about my mother's condition, I drank more. Then I saw an advertisement for an apple flavored vodka. So I just had to try it and see if it tasted like the apple flavored beer I was drinking. The next couple of years it became my best friend at night. Trying to deal with my mother's sickness and the drinking I became a very miserable person.

One of my co-workers told me at that time in my life I was almost evil early in the morning. But by the middle of the morning on I was okay. That did not prove well for my act of faith at that time in my life. James 2:26 (KJV) *For as the body without the spirit is dead, so faith without works is dead also.* Which only goes to prove the saying if we talk the talk we better walk the walk. People around us see our actions not our faith. Faith comes from within us, and no one else knows about it but yourself. At times in our lives we can bury our faith deep inside of ourselves. But the actions we do because of our faith in God other people see.

From that point until my mother's physical death here on earth and her going to be with the Lord, I do not remember much about my life (if you would call it life). The last few months of my mother's life here on earth I called her every week. I could not hear her voice, only mumbles on the phone as she tried to talk to her son who was so far away. It broke my heart every time I listened to her, not only because it was hard for her to try and talk, but because I knew that might be the last time I would hear her on the phone.

When I was forty-six, in January of 2005, I received a phone call from my older sister, Brenda, that my mother had passed away and was now with the Lord. You think that you will be ready when the phone call comes with the news, but I was not. Not since the death of my friend Terry when I was nineteen had I felt so hopeless. I had not lost anyone else so dear to my heart to death. All these years God had been so merciful to our families. Diana or I had not lost any immediate family members. With the news I had to make a decision that was very hard for me. My mother was being taken care at home by her husband and my siblings, along with the help and support of hospice. My mother, wanting to be a help to others, she gave her body to science in hopes they might find a cure or better treatments to help others with cancer. So in light of this, there was not going to be a funeral but a memorial service instead.

I so much wanted to be there but it was the middle of January, bad winter weather could pop up at any time. All of our children wanted to go but not all of them could take off work long enough to travel to Mississippi and back. Two of our children were living across the state from us, which was a five hour drive just to get here before we could leave on a trip. My in-laws were concerned obviously for the weather conditions but Beva, my mother-in-law, told Diana and me to pray about it, she would pray about it and see how the Lord would lead us in this situation. She said that she would support us in whatever decision we came up with. So I did pray about it and came to the conclusion to stay in Pennsylvania. We would have a memorial service for my mother here. If we stayed here at least all of our children and grandchildren would be able to attend along with our family here and close friends.

I made the call to Brenda and explained the situation to her. I told her we would not be making the trip back home. She was disappointed but said she understood. My mother's third husband, whom she was married to since 2000, was very upset we were not coming. But I had to do what I felt was best not only for me but my family also. Now I had to find someone to do the memorial service for my mother here in Pennsylvania. We had not been attending church for almost three years now, so I felt awkward asking the pastor at our former church to do a service for my mother. And I am sure he would have done it, but we did not know him very well. He was attending there while we were going but became the pastor after we stop attending church services there. So I had to make a decision because I wanted to have our memorial service the same day and time as the one my family was having in Mississippi if at all possible.

In the past year the church where my in-laws attended and where Diana and I were married was no longer available. The church had become such a small congregation it struggled financially. So they decided to be joined with the First Baptist Church some eight miles away into one congregation. And so that was where my in-laws were attending church services. I called my mother-in-law and asked her if she thought her pastor would do a memorial service for my mother. She told me she would contact him explain the situation to him and see what he said. Not very long after we talked, she called me back. She said her pastor agreed to do it and wanted me to call him. I called him, explained the situation, and agreed to meet him the next day with as many of my children as possible. He said for us to think about things we remembered about my mother, what she liked, hymns she liked, some of her favorite Bible verses if we knew what they were.

The next day we met Pastor Dave for the first time. We talked about my mothers life, and the memorial service. My mother loved to bake, liked to watch sports on TV, and cooked for her local high school football team on Fridays. We laughed, we cried, and Pastor Dave prayed for us.

I called my sister and let her know that the memorial service here in Pennsylvania was set for January 18, 2005 at 7:00 pm. It was to be on the same day and the same time as the one they were having in Mississippi. The service was attended by our family and close friends. Opening scripture reading was from Proverbs 3:5-6 (KJV) *Thrust in the Lord with all thine heart; and lean not unto thine own understanding. In all thy ways acknowledge him, and he shall direct thy paths.* We sang *Blessed Assurance,* there was the eulogy by Pastor Dave and a time for us to talk about my mother.

This part of the service was very hard, but also very helpful in the healing process of our souls. The ones of us that did share about my mother cried almost the entire time we spoke. I shared many things about my mother in between my tears but at the end of my speech I shared a poem I had written my mother four years earlier. Time had slipped away so quickly that at one point a seven-year period had gone by without a visit to Mississippi. We talked on the phone but had not seen each other face to face. I penned this poem and read it to my mother the first day of our visit in November of 2001 after that seven-year period.

> The love of a mother, the love of a son
> the love between them cannot be undone.
> The years they had passed, so quickly away
> I couldn't stay away, not for one more day.
> Plans had been made, plans had been broken
> my mother I was seeing my words had been spoken.
> Oh what a day that was for me
> at last my mother I finally did see.
> The joy in her face as she looked at mine

my it had been a long, long time.
A tear on her cheek, a smile on my face
this moment in time can't be replaced.
The love of a mother, the love of a son
with them together their bond was as one.

And with every line I read tears just kept pouring down my face as I realized I would not see my mother any more this side of heaven. We sang *How Great Thou Art*. Pastor Dave gave a message and prayed for the family. We sang *Amazing Grace*. Then the committal was read from the twenty-third and forty-six Psalm. We had a collage of photos set up on a table for everyone to look at along with some books my mother had given me. One in particular, *White Trash Cookbook*, Pastor Dave's brother Brian thought was amusing. He played the music for the memorial service.

After talking for a while we thanked Pastor Dave for doing the service and asked what we owed him for doing the service for us. He just look at me in the eyes and said, "You do not owe me anything I'm glad I could do it for you. I do have one request though. I would like to invite you to come back on Sundays and worship with us." He knew from our previous conversations that we were not going to church anywhere at that present time. I told him we would think about it and left.

The next couple of days Diana and I talked it over and decide to at least go there Sunday morning since Pastor Dave did the memorial service for us. Plus the fact that Diana's mother and father were in their late seventies and early eighties and we were not sure how much longer they would be with us on earth either.

Sunday morning came. We got up and got ready for church. We were met at the door with friendly faces. As we walked in and found them we surprised her mother and father. My father-in-law just looked at us in shock but Diana and her mother both had tears streaming down their faces. As the Sunday service began you could tell there was something different. It was not a traditional Baptist service. There were lead singers up front with an organ player, piano player, guitar player, and a drummer, and they were singing songs from a projector screen. No hymns were being sung from hymnals. I looked around and there were several senior citizens in attendance, and they were singing right along. A few of them were even clapping every now and then.

Then the time came for Pastor Dave to give his message. To be honest I do not remember at all what verses from the Bible he used or what he preached about. But I do remember this: I liked it. I did not fall asleep and he wasn't banging on a pulpit. He just kept your attention on what he was preaching. Pastor Dave wove real life stories in and out through his message. All in all Diana and I both liked the church service.

The next week our middle son Nicholas and his family joined us at church. They had been thinking about going to church and this just seemed like a good time to start. A couple of months later our oldest son Matthew and his daughter Haley began attending church with us also. As the weeks went by you could see the happiness we had brought to Diana's mother. She told us some time later how God had answered her prayer and brought us back to the church. And knowing my mother-in-law the way I do. I know for sure that she spent many nights while we were away from the church praying for our return. Proverbs 15:29 says, "The Lord is far from the wicked but he hears the prayer of the righteous."

Now we had been going to church for several weeks and the mending process of my soul back to the Lord was coming along, but I had not given up the bottle yet. I was still drinking every night but not as much on Saturday as before. Now in the spring of that year Diana and I decided to join the church. We went to a class on a

Saturday that Pastor Dave gives to people who either are joining the church or being baptized. After the teaching session we who were joining the church met with the deacons and Pastor Dave to give them a testimony about ourselves.

My turn was a little long winded because, well, I like to talk; what can I say. My wife's turn was after me and I remember her saying, "You expect me to follow him?" But she did and in her testimony and also in mine Pastor Dave found out that we had sung on the praise team at the last church we attended. So from then on every Sunday when shaking his hand after the church service Pastor Dave asked us to join the praise team. We just looked at him said we would think about it and left it at that.

Now I had started reading my Bible again, not every day but at least more than just on Sundays. God was changing my heart back to him slowly but surely a little bit at a time day by day.

We had been struggling financially for some time by then; Diana was having a hard time with the bills each month. We knew to get our finances straightened out we needed to give more than five dollars to the church each week. As we prayed and started relying more and more on the Lord for guidance, we began tithing to the church. I decided we needed to get rid of some of our boats we had four so we sold three of them. And that helped out tremendously.

I went into the hospital for my third checkup on my throat. The first two times I had it checked, the results were basically the same. I would go to the hospital, the doctor would do the procedure, she would tell us it looked ok, but she took scrapes of my throat to make sure I did not have cancer. Then she would call me with the results of the test and say I'll check it again in three years.

This time that was not the phone call I received. The doctor saw something in the pictures of my throat and in the cultures she did not like. So instead of taking one pill a day for my acid reflux, now I was to begin taking two a day and my doctor wanted to do the test over again not in three years, not even one year, but in six months. And she wanted me to quit chewing tobacco and stop drinking alcoholic beverages. Now that made Diana and me concerned but we tried not to think about it too much.

After Pastor Dave's persistence every week asking us to join the praise team, we decided to go to a praise practice and see what it was like. We also wanted to get to know some of the worship leaders a little better. While at the meeting Pastor Dave said that the leadership of the church needs to be walking the walk and not just talking the talk. He said I may not know how your walk is or what you might be doing that is not appropriate for leaders of the church to be involved in, but God knew. And God knew that was exactly what I needed to hear. We sang with the praise team. I went home and stopped drinking the next day. Now that not only helped me spiritually and physically, but that helped us financially also.

I began watching the Christian channel, Cornerstone, on TV almost exclusively. Sometimes I would watch the Food channel or the History channel but mostly the Christian channel. All of the Christian teaching and Christian programs helped in changing my life for the better. I just couldn't get enough of Christian programming. I began turning off my radio in my truck on my ride to work and my ride home. Every day I spent that time with the Lord, besides my bedtime talk and little talks throughout the day. If you want your life to change for the better, if you want your relationship with the Lord to grow spend more time in prayer.

A month or so after I had stopped drinking on my ride to work I told the Lord, I surrender my life all of it to you. All that I am I owe to you so my life is yours if you want it. I also told him he could use me in his service in any way he saw fit. That afternoon when I got home there was a message on the answering machine from Don, one of the members of our church. I called him back and he wanted me to consider becoming a deacon at the church. I said I would pray about it but I would like to talk to Pastor Dave about it.

I made an appointment with Pastor Dave and we talked for about an hour and a half. When I was done telling him my life's story he asked me, "How is your walk with the Lord right now?"

And I told him, "Great."

He said, "That's good enough for me."

I told him I would bring him a video of me preaching that he might get a laugh out of because I had very long hair back then.

The next week he watched the tape and told me that if he went away on a Sunday sometime they could just play the tape in church. Then he said, "Oh, better yet, I'll just have you preach." I laughed. Pastor Dave smiled and he said, "I'm serious," and I left it at that. With all of these things going on in my life I noticed I was no longer miserable at work.

By the time I was forty-seven I had become good friends with a co-worker over the last twelve months. He had noticed the change from the grumpy hung-over drunk he worked with a year before, to a person who was living life to the Lord one day at a time. I was allowing God to do his work in me. I would tell my co-worker, whose nickname is Hook, about the Lord, tell him about the church, and about Pastor Dave. I asked him to come to church but he would just politely brush me off.

Actions do speak louder than words. We were having a drama preformed at our church and Diana and I were going to help lead the singing so I kept asking Hook to come. He finally gave in and said he would come and bring his wife Anna.

The first night of the drama Hook and Anna went forward to the altar call. Hook rededicated his life to the Lord and his wife Anna asked Jesus to be her savior. When I saw them go forward I just began to cry. Because of my returning to the Lord and living a life for him letting God change my life in front of my co-worker, now he was surrendering his life back to the Lord and his wife was now a child of God. They returned the next two nights and saw her dad accept Jesus as his savior and someone else they invited to rededicate his life to the Lord. We had another co-worker Walt come with his family. His stepdaughter and his grandson accepted the Lord as their savior that night. And my son, Nicholas and his wife rededicated their lives to the Lord and some of his wife's family asked Jesus to either become their savior or rededicated their lives to the Lord. The next Sunday there were three pews full of friends and family coming to church with us. Hallelujah!

Hook and I began listening to music CDs from church or CDs we had bought of contemporary Christian music. Every day at work we were singing and smiling a lot. God had put so much joy in our lives we could hardly stand it. Now I understood what Paul was writing about in Philippians 2:1-5, "If you have any encouragement from being united with Christ, if any comfort from his love, if any fellowship with the Spirit, if any tenderness and compassion, then make my joy complete by being like-minded, having the same love, being one in spirit and purpose. Do nothing out of selfish ambition or vain conceit, but in humility consider others better than yourselves. Each of you should look not only to your interests, but also to the interests of others. Your attitude should be the same as that of Christ Jesus." My joy was not only in the Lord but in the fact that because I was living a life for the Lord now I had the joy of knowing my co-worker, my friend, my brother in Christ was living in that same joy of the Lord.

In November Diana and I went to a Bible study a church group was having at a fire hall four nights a week. It lasted for six weeks. That just made me hungrier for the word of God. I also decided to put my motorcycle up for sale. Since we were going back to church we were not riding it any longer. We still owed more than half of the money on the bike. But I wanted to get rid of that payment each month. I put it up for sale and I had people tell me, "Its winter, you will never get your money out of it," but I really wasn't worried about that. I just wanted rid of it so we were not making payments on something we did not use anymore. We put an ad in a local newspaper and after the first week we had no calls. People would ask me if I had sold it yet. I would tell them no, not yet, and they would say to me again, "You will not sell it now for what you need to pay it off, it is winter time."

We checked the paper we had put the ad in and did not see the ad, so we thought the money did not get there in time for that week and that was the reason for no calls. The next week when the paper came we looked again and still no ad. Diana called the paper and they told her it was in the week before. We rechecked and they were correct there it was in black and white. But we had no calls on it. I just left it in the Lord's hands. He knew I didn't need the motorcycle and I was trying to get a better hold on our finances.

About a week later I got a phone call. Someone's friend had seen the ad in the paper and saved it for him. He wanted to know if I still had the motorcycle. I told him yes. He came and looked at the bike and asked me what was the lowest price I would take for it. I told him and he said he would think about it. One or two days went by. He called me up and said he would take it. I not only sold it for the price to pay it off, but I made $500 extra.

The Monday after Thanksgiving we went back to the hospital to have another throat scope done and to have some more cultures taken. After the procedure the doctor said everything looks about the same and that her office would call us with the results in a few days. A week went by and we had not received any calls from the doctor's office. By the end of the next week Diana was getting a little concerned. By the third week now I was starting to be alarmed a bit. Things started going through my mind about my mother. How she had died less than a year ago from throat cancer. The next thing I knew I was feeling sick, and I just knew in my mind I had cancer for certain. Until one day on my way to work I just left it in the Lord's hands. I told the Lord listen for almost thirty-two years I have chewed tobacco, if I have throat cancer it is nobody's fault but my own. I take full responsibility for that. But I know that if I have cancer you, Lord, if you are willing can heal my cancer. I felt a peace come over me after that prayer and did not think any more negative thoughts after that. A couple of more days went by and Diana told me to just call the doctor's office when I got home and see what they said. I called the doctor's office and they told me, "Oh, Mr. Bowman, we are so sorry. We thought someone had already called you. Everything is fine. Stay on your medicine. The doctor will see you in three years." Oh what a relief for my wife and myself.

In December Diana and myself were asked to lead a Sunday school class for twelve weeks on financial principles. Here we were just recovering from money problems ourselves, and they wanted us to lead a class on money. God knows us better than we know ourselves. We learned so much from that class. The two biggest things I learned from the class were these: God owns everything and we are the stewards. In Psalm 24:1, "The earth is the Lord's, and everything in it, the world, and all who live in it." And that we should give sometimes sacrificially to God's purposes, helping the poor, feeding the hungry, and helping others who are just in need.

In Mark 12:41-44, "Jesus sat down opposite the place where the offerings were put and watched the crowds putting their money in the temple treasury. Many rich people threw in large amounts. But a poor widow came and put in two very small copper coins, worth only a fraction of a penny. Calling his disciples to him, Jesus said, 'I tell you the truth, this poor widow has put more into the treasury than all the others. They all gave out of their wealth; but she, out of her poverty, put in everything-all she had to live on."

Also in December Pastor Dave had a sermon on crossing over bridges and not looking back. I decided after that message that I would quit chewing tobacco. My wife had asked me to quit chewing, my doctor had asked me to stop chewing, but I wouldn't. But it seemed like two or three preachers on TV that week also hit home about my chewing tobacco. That same week I began to think on how I used to hear from God but he had not spoken to me in years. And the last time I remember hearing from God I was not chewing tobacco, because I had quit when I was preaching years ago. And I'm not talking about hearing from God in the scriptures, or the feeling inside we get when we do things that God would have us to do. I'm talking about God's Spirit, the Holy Spirit living inside of me talking to my spirit. Actually hearing the Holy Spirit speaking to me. That is how God used to talk to me sometimes and I miss that. Does or will God speak to everyone like that I don't know, that is just how he has talked to me from time to time.

All I know is when God talked to me before I was not chewing tobacco. In 1 Corinthians 6:19-20, "Do you not know that your body is a temple of the Holy Spirit, who is in you, whom you have received from God? You are not your own; you were bought at a price. Therefore honor God with your body." This scripture also helped me to come to the decision to stop chewing tobacco. I finished the pack of chewing tobacco I had and did not buy any more. I asked my mother-in-law to pray for me, and I shared with the praise team at practice my decision to stop chewing. Of course I received lots of support. When I decided to stop chewing tobacco Jesus and his wilderness temptations came to mind. I looked them up in the Bible and noticed every time Satan tempted Jesus he would quote scripture, and Satan moved on to another temptation until finally Satan gave up and left Jesus alone.

So I used Jesus as my example and found a couple of scriptures that I thought fit my situation and tried it out. Every time I felt an urge to have a chew I would quote Philippians 4:13 (KJV) *I can do All things through Christ who strengheneth me.* And also 1 John 4:4 (KJV) *Greater is He that is in you than he that is in the world.* It was like a miracle. The urge would leave immediately after I said those scriptures. Then after awhile the urge would come back and I would repeat the scriptures again and the urge would go away again. This went on for two weeks. After that no more urges to chew that was it done deal. Thank you Jesus.

In January our daughter Sarah was to be giving birth to our fourth grandchild. She did not go to church with us but she knew God and she knew Diana and I were both trying to live a life pleasing to the Lord. We talked on the phone on a Sunday evening and she was ready to give birth. But the baby wasn't ready to be born. She was a week overdue and just wanted the baby to be born. Before we ended our conversation she asked if I would please ask God to let her have her baby soon. I agreed to pray that she would have her baby soon. That evening before bed I made a special request on behalf of my daughter.

The next evening I was watching Cornerstone, the Christian channel as usual and Diana was nodding off on the couch. They were having a telethon to raise money for the Christian channel I watch. They were trying to get people during that part of the telethon to give one-time gifts of different amounts. God put a figure on my heart I felt he wanted me to give. I sat there for almost an hour watching Diana nodding off, when I finally could not take it anymore. She kind of came to and I told her I felt God wanted us to give $100 to the TV station. She said, "Okay, did you call yet?" and I told her no, I was waiting for her to wake up. I called the TV station and gave them my pledge of $100.

The next day after work Diana called me at home and said, "Sarah is in the hospital." She said that she was in labor and not to get to excited. There was plenty of time for Diana to come home from work and then we would go to the hospital. Diana got home from work, we ate supper real fast and were leaving for the hospital. The phone rang. It was Sarah's friend who was with her at the hospital telling us to get there soon. We hopped in the car, got to the hospital twenty minutes away and we saw her for thirty minutes before she was to deliver. Forty minutes later she was holding her son they were both fine.

Did I buy an answer to my prayer? No, of course not. You cannot buy God's favors. I believe God had mercy on my daughter and answered my prayer because I was faithful to make that pledge I felt God asked me to give. I was obedient to God's call. We had not sent the money in yet; I had only pledged to give it. We did not mail the money for another two weeks after we received a pledge card in the mail.

I had a note pad in my desk at work I had written Philippians 4:13 and 1 John 4:4 on it to read when I would have an urge to chew. I took that pad and on the left side of the page I wrote **Acts of the Sinful Nature**, from Galatians chapter 5 which are, "sexual immorality, impurity, debauchery, idolatry, witchcraft, hatred, discord, jealousy, fits of rage, selfish ambition, dissensions, fractions, envy, drunkenness, and orgies." On the other side of the page I wrote **the Fruits of the Spirit,** which are, "Love, Joy, Peace, Patience, Kindness, Gentleness, and Self-Control." I would look at that page a few times throughout the day and say to myself *I do not want to do these.* Then read the list of sinful acts. Then I would read the Fruits of the Spirit and say to myself, *May these grow in me.* And some of the fruit had already been growing but I wanted bigger fruit and more of them. Jesus said in Matthew 7:17-18, "Likewise every good tree bears good fruit, but a bad tree bears bad fruit. A good tree cannot bear bad fruit, and a bad tree cannot bear good fruit." Throughout the Bible people are symbolized as trees. What kind of fruit are you producing Good fruit or Bad fruit?

I have been reading my Bible or Bible stories as long as I can remember with the exceptions of the backsliding periods of my life. I had only ever read completely all the way through the Bible once. But watching the Christian channel on TV and reading my Bible daily I was still hungry for the word of God. I just could not get enough.

I had on cassette tapes the King James Version of the Bible. Hook and I began listening to music in the morning and then we would listen to the Bible tapes in the afternoon. We were so excited and hungry for the word we just could not get enough of it. We would be listening to the tapes and all of a sudden one of us would say, "Stop, did you hear that?" Then we would rewind it, play it again and discuss what we had just listened to. It took about three weeks to go through the Old Testament and a week and a half to go through the New Testament.

While going through the Bible on cassette, I shared with a small group at church that we were listening to the Bible at work but I wish I had one of the newer versions to also listen too. One of the group members I shared this with, Ardath, told me she had bought the New Testament on cassette off of an internet auction for $10 and the tapes were dramatized. They had different people speaking the different parts and you could hear background sounds also. Then she asked if I would like to try them at work and of course I said, "Yes."

I borrowed them from her and after listening to one of them at home I asked my wife Diana to get online and find me a set of those tapes on the whole Bible. Diana found me a set for around $30 and I had them in about two weeks. While waiting on my set of tapes I took the ones I borrowed to work. Hook and I couldn't hardly wait to listen to the tapes each day. People would walk by our work area and say, "What are you listening to?"

Hook or I would say, "The Bible," then there were different answers we got back like. "Oh," or "Cool," or "Why?" Shortly after getting my tapes Hook got moved to another part of our plant. The line we worked on had slowed down. I was upset when he first got moved but I came to the conclusion that God just wanted us to spread the word and God's love to a different part of the plant. For a few weeks I listened to the music and the Bible mostly by myself with the exception of one of my other co-workers, John who listened to the Bible with me.

Chapter Seven

*I*n February Diana and I had gone to lunch after church with her parents, Beva and Joe, her brother Bob, his wife Lorna, and their son Clint. Also a couple we know from church, Dean and his wife Tricia sat down at the table with us. We asked them where their two girls were? They said the girls had gone with their grandparents after church so the couple could eat out by themselves. Valentine's Day was coming up and this was their chance to eat alone, they told us. While we were having our lunch I felt in my heart God wanted me to pay for their lunch. We were having lunch at a China Buffet and on one of our trips to the buffet I told Diana I felt like God wanted me to pay for their lunch. Was it okay with her? She said, "Yes you can pay for their lunch if you have enough money on you."

When the waitress passed out the bills I said to Dean, "Can I see your bill?" Without really thinking about it he handed it to me. I looked at it, looked at him and said, "Lunch is on my wife and I."

He looked at me like I was nuts and said, "No, that's ok."

I told him, "No, I would like to pay for your lunch."

He said, "No really you don't have to."

I told him, "Listen, God wants me to pay for your meal okay?"

He just smiled then and said, "Okay thanks."

I said, "You're welcome."

We were faithfully going to church every week. Our Sunday school class on money was over but most of the class members continued on with us as we began a discipleship class. I was studying the Word at home, listening to the music, listening to the Bible at work, and just living life to its full.

Don't get me wrong, not everything was a bed of roses, I had some struggles too. Something happened at work that really upset me. Now what happened doesn't really matter, but I got very upset with a couple of my co-workers. They had said something that I did not like and I was not happy about it. I didn't say anything to them but they knew I was mad about something. God knew I was mad, he knows everything. After work that day and that evening, the more I thought about it the madder I got. The next day on my way to work I was praying to God as usual when half way through my prayer time God interrupted me and said, "You have to forgive them."

Without even thinking I said right back, "I don't want to."

Now I'm not talking about some feelings I had in my heart here. I was right in the middle of talking to God in prayer when he interrupted me. That in itself was a miracle for me one that I had been looking forward to, hearing God's voice again. But just when I finally did hear from God what did I do? I argued with him. But it was short-lived because God said right back to me. "I forgave you; I want you to forgive them." You cannot argue with that you just can't.

So when I got to work I walked up to my two co-workers and said, "Good morning."

They said to me, "Aren't you mad anymore?"

I told them, "Nope, I'm over it."

We came home from church one Sunday. As I went upstairs I noticed the sound of water running in the wall. I ran right back downstairs into the basement and shut off the water supply. As I made it back upstairs, the kitchen floor was soaked, the kitchen ceiling was soaking wet, and my ceiling fan light globe was full of water. Now if that had happened a little over a year before that I would have been stomping my feet, screaming and hollering and probably saying a few unchoice words. But as I stood there on that day I looked at everything and said, "Lord, it's your house, do with it as you will."

Sounds kind of silly, I know, but we had just recently gone through the class on money principles. In that class we learned that God owns everything. We are his stewards; we just use them. So with this kind of a mindset that's why I said, "Lord it's your house, do with it as you will."

Diana and I cleaned the water on the floor up, I took the globe down, and emptied the water out of it. Then we waited two days. The ceiling fan and light had dried out and the ceiling tile dried up. The ceiling tile did not fall down, the floor did not buckle up, and the ceiling fan and light both worked. We only had to pay for a plumber to fix the broken pipe. Proverbs 3:5 says, "Trust in the Lord with all your heart and lean not on your own understanding." We trust God with our lives, we trust God with our eternity, shouldn't we trust God with our possessions he allows us to use?

A few weeks later I was watching one of the preachers I like on the Christian channel. It was about three weeks before Easter Sunday. He was saying how every Easter his church takes up a special offering. A sacrificial offering they had been taking up many years. Then he showed a film clip of the first year they did it and the preacher was in his early twenties. He wanted people to give a whole week's paycheck as that offering. He said how God would give those people who gave this sacrificial offering a special blessing and could also expect a resurrection miracle. He said that Jesus at Easter had given the best sacrificial offering that could ever be given. Jesus gave himself for our sins. He gave his life so that we might have life.

Now I was watching this program. It was ok, but I wasn't getting too uplifted by this talk of wanting this offering. This offering was not just to come from his local church but from all his TV viewers. This man is one of the Big preachers of our time. He has a huge church, a Bible college, overseas ministries, I mean he is Big.

But I just wasn't really interested in hearing anymore about that offering. I was ready for him to move on and get to his message, when suddenly God spoke to me his Spirit to my spirit and said, "I want you to do that."

I said, "You want me to give a whole week's pay to that preacher on TV."

God said, "No, I want you to give it to the Kingdom."

"Oh, okay," I replied. Now I'm thinking to myself, *what did I just agree to do? I said I would give a whole week's pay to the kingdom. What part of the kingdom? Was I to give this money to the TV preacher or not?*

Well, I said nothing to Diana about this until I could try and figure out what I was supposed to do with the money I agreed to give to the kingdom. So I prayed about it and prayed about it and prayed about it. This went on for two weeks and I had still not told my wife. Diana takes care of all our finances. I needed to tell her but tell her what exactly I wasn't sure. The last week, the week before Easter, I was on my ride home from work when I began to think to myself. *I could take that paycheck and pay our boat dock fees for the year instead of giving it to the kingdom.* But by the time I made it home I realized that was just the carnal side of me, trying to talk the spiritual side me out of doing what God had asked of me. But I had to tell my wife. Time was running out.

Diana came home from work; I asked how her day was. It hadn't been the best day, as a matter of fact it wasn't a good day at all. So I didn't say anything about the offering. After we ate supper I stood and looked at the calendar we have hanging on the wall in the dining room. I was looking to see if we both got paid that week or just me. Diana gets paid every other week and I get paid every week.

As I was looking at the calendar Diana asked me, "What are you looking at?"

I told her I was seeing if we both got paid or just me. She said, "We both are getting paid. Why?"

There was my opening to tell her my plans. I said, "God has told me to give my whole paycheck this week to him." It's hard for me to put into words the reaction I received from my wife. This is the woman who has supported me positively in everything I have done concerning God.

But Diana looked at me in a way I had never seen before and she yelled, "Are you crazy? Our church is not hurting for money! And I have bills every month I need to pay."

I said nothing, went into the living room, and left her alone in the dining room. I sat there in my chair watching TV and began praying, *Lord I need some help here. I want to do what you told me to do but I need Diana to agree with me on this.* God had already helped us come out of our money problems. I just needed Diana to trust me and trust God in this situation.

After about fifteen minutes Diana came into the living room. She told me she was sorry for acting the way she did. She had a very bad day at work and she wasn't expecting me to say anything like that. I explained to her how God had asked me to give my paycheck to the kingdom.

Diana said, "Are we giving it all to our church?"

I told her, "No, I have been praying about it and finally had decided on giving our church half of my paycheck, buying some Bibles for a missionary project at church, another local church was starting a Christian school, and I wanted to send another check to the Cornerstone TV station I was always watching.

Diana liked my idea, so we sat down and figured out how much to give to everyone. Then we began to get happy about giving it away. By the time Easter Sunday got here we were overjoyed to give my paycheck to the kingdom. I had not worked any overtime at my job for almost three months. The week after Easter I worked overtime for three weeks in a row and not only did I make my paycheck back but, I made a little extra too. Then I did not work any overtime for another two months. Coincidental? I think not. The money did not fall out of the sky. Deuteronomy 8:18 says, "But remember the Lord your God, for it is he who gives you the ability to produce wealth." I was able to earn my money back from my job. God knows our every need. God knew we had bills to pay. He was testing me to see if I would do what he had asked me to do. Did I receive a special blessing like the TV preacher said I would? Yes we did, and the special blessing we received was one of joy in knowing we did something God had asked us to do. Not only that but he also said we would receive a resurrection miracle also. I will share about that miracle later on.

I noticed on the bulletin board at church the youth group was going to have a lock-in. A lock-in is where usually the youth of the church together with adult leaders and chaperones stay overnight or a couple of days and nights together. During this time together they will pray, read God's word and do all kinds of activities together to draw one another closer to God and each other.

At first I didn't think much about it, but the closer it got to the actual time for the lock-in I began to feel like God wanted me to go and be a part of it. The Wednesday night before the weekend the lock-in was to happen I told Diana on the way to praise practice I thought God wanted me to go to the lock-in. She said whatever I thought I should do just go ahead and do it. Before practice I told Pastor Dave I felt like God wanted me to go to the youth lock-in. I thought I might get questioned on why I might think that but Pastor Dave just began jumping up and down and said, "Yes, yes!"

I thought to myself, *Chill out, man, it's not that big of a deal.*

Later on that evening I told our drummer, Dave, who himself and his wife, Wendy, were helping with the youth group. He said, cool, but he needed to tell the person in charge of the lock-in, Janet. She just happened to drop by a little later. Dave talked with her and Janet said that would be great.

I have never been to a lock-in but our children used to go when they were in youth group at church. I knew they usually stayed up all night doing all kinds of activities. We had that past January bought a ping pong table and our neighbors, Keith and Helen, would come over and we would play four or five nights a week. I knew there was a ping pong table at church so I decided to take my own paddles and some balls just in case they didn't have any. I figured when there was a break in the scheduled activities we could play some ping pong. I thought to myself I could probably show them a thing or two on the table. I wasn't a pro, not by a long shot, but I was pretty good at it. Also Diana had bought me a DVD Bible Trivia game that had three levels. That I also was going to take along. I had played it several times and I was pretty good at it, too. As a matter of a fact I had not missed a question, I was perfect on level one, ages 0-8.

By the time Saturday night came I was pumped up. When I arrived I found out they had activities scheduled from 9:00 that night till 12:00 noon the next day. So much for my DVD Trivia game or my showing off at ping pong.

As the night began Dave, the drummer, did not act as though he was having a good time and it had just started. He told me if he did not hear from God that night he was done helping with youth group. Every chance we got he would talk to me. He was also talking with one of the other youth leaders. I gave hardly any advice at all. Mostly I just listened. We all made it through the night and to church the next morning with only a couple of hours of sleep. I had a great time getting to know the youth leaders and the youth of the church better. When I left church that Sunday I had not played ping pong the night before or Bible Trivia. But I had obeyed the Lord and had a great time doing it.

The next Wednesday I talked with Dave at praise practice. He said to me, "Wendy and I know why God wanted you to be at the lock-in." It was so he would have someone to talk to, someone who had time to just listen to him. When God asks us to do things, sometimes it is not about us. I had all these plans of things I wanted to do that night but God had another plan, and his was better. I'm glad I listened to my heart and went to that lock-in. It's like the hymn whose words ring out: "Trust and Obey for there is no other way but to be happy in Jesus but to trust and obey."

Diana woke me one morning to get ready for work. While I was getting ready I remembered a dream I had during the night. So I went downstairs and told Diana my dream. We both thought it was different and a little humorous. I even went to work and told some of my co-workers about it and they would laugh and say you are not right, which I agreed with them, of course.

My dream was an animated dream about fishing, again. This time I was fishing with two talking dogs. The one dog was a spunky little border collie. It would not be still. He was on the go throughout the whole dream. The other dog was a big bulldog with the big floppy cheeks. Now he was actually fishing with me on the bank above a huge gully. We had baited our hooks and threw the lines blindly out into the gully. We were sitting a ways back from the edge of the bank waiting patiently for a bite. The whole time we sat there fishing the big bulldog talked. He talked and talked and talked. I couldn't get a word in edge ways if I had wanted to, but I really was content just listening and taking in all the big bulldog had to say.

All of a sudden we heard the little dog off at a distant saying, "You might get a bite if you put your bait in the water." I stood up walk over to the edge and looked. Our fishing lines and the bait were not even close to any water, they were laying on dry ground. There was a dam in the gully about fifty yards away where all the water was backed up.

Just like the other fishing dream I kept thinking about it over and over. It would just pop into my head at any time. And this went on for a few weeks until finally I just asked God, "Are you trying to tell me something from this fishing dream also, like you did with the other fishing dream I had? If so you need to shine some light on it for me because I'm not figuring it out on my own." Then one morning I woke up and had my answer. The water was the world; my testimony about Jesus in my life was the bait. And I had to stop just sitting around listening to God's word through other people all the time. It was time for me to share my testimony about Jesus with others. I was studying the word of God and watching a lot of Christian TV but I was holding all this information to myself. I needed to share it with others, not just keep it for myself.

So I tried sharing at work but it was hard. I had been so used to sharing with Hook but since he was moved to a different area in my plant there was not really anyone else that I worked with who cared to hear about the Lord. I shared with John some and with Don, one of my other Christian co-workers, but that wasn't exactly what God meant for me to do. One of my other co-workers said he believed in God but just not the way I do. I just did not know what to do about my situation.

A couple of weeks before the Memorial Day weekend Pastor Dave ask Diana and me if we wanted to go camping with them. We said yes and I could hardly wait for that weekend to arrive. I was excited to be spending a long weekend with Pastor Dave and his family to become better acquainted with them.

Finally Memorial Day weekend arrived and we got to the campground on Friday evening and set up camp. Pastor Dave and his family arrived shortly thereafter. Pastor Dave and his family got their campsite set up. Pastor Dave started a fire in his four foot fire ring he brought himself so we could get supper going. We sat around the fire eating and talking, something we Baptists like to do. Eat and talk, talk and eat, they just go hand in hand. As the evening went on and our conversations headed toward talking about the church some, Pastor Dave asked me a question I was not really expecting from him. He asked me if I would consider preaching in his place while he and his family went on vacation in three weeks. I was a little shocked at first but I should not have been. He had warned me a few months earlier that he would like for me to fill in for him sometime. But I guess in my mind I thought he was really just kidding. And that Sunday just happens to be Father's Day, too, something to consider with the subject matter that I might preach on.

After that the rest of the evening was back to talking about camping and other non-church talk. Really just getting to know each other a little better than the way we see each other at church. We talked about family, friends, jobs, and hobbies. The next day we were going out on Pastor Dave's sailboat. I had never been on a sailboat, just about every other kind of a boat but not a sailboat.

Pastor Dave was telling me about the time he flipped the sailboat, how he was hoping the wind would pick up so we could sail quickly across the lake that day. But after hearing the boat flipping story I was praying, *Nice and calm Lord, nice and calm.*

That day the Lord answered my prayer and the winds were just moderate, just enough to move us along at a gentle pace. That first trip out was just Pastor Dave and I alone we got to know just a little bit more about each other. For about an hour and a half Pastor Dave and I talked one on one. It was the high point of my weekend, just sharing with each other real life testimonies. Things we had done in our lives we were not too proud of and things we had done that we were proud of, encouraging one another.

As Christians we do not do this enough. Romans 1:12 says, "that you and I may be mutually encouraged by each other's faith." Christian fellowship builds up our faith. When we talk with other Christians and see how they have been through some of the same trials or tribulations and survived, we are encouraged. Then we begin to think there is hope for me after all. Maybe I can live through this thing, whatever it might be, after all. People do not like to let others know their faults or their disappointments. We do not want others to know where we are or have been vulnerable. It is just not in our natural makeup. We have to draw it out from within. And we do that through the power of the Holy Spirit.

While Pastor Dave and I were on the sailboat, Diana was spending time with his wife, Brenda, and their two daughters, Shelby and Abby. That evening Pastor Dave had invited several people from church to the campground for supper and fellowship. There was lots of good food.

Pastor Dave asked me to say grace over the food and I remember thinking to myself, *Okay, try and keep it simple.* So I prayed, "Father thank you for the food, the fun, and the fellowship. Amen." Then I said, "Let's eat" and everyone kind of laughed and we commenced to eating. While at the table during all the conversations going on, Pastor Dave announced that I would be preaching in his place on Father's Day while he and his family were away on vacation. The people were probably as shocked as I was at first. I imagined them thinking, *This fellow just said one of the shortest blessings over our food that we have ever heard. Pastor Dave's going to let him preach. We will be out early that Sunday morning. Or what kind of a sermon will this Mississippi-raised hillbilly preach on and will we be able to understand him? He talks kind of funny.* But they all gave encouraging words. With the exception of the ones there that night who went on vacation with the pastor and his family, they were all present on that Father's Day morning service to support me. By the time that Memorial Day weekend was over, Diana and I did not want to leave.

It had nothing to do with the time we had spent with Pastor Dave and his family, well maybe it did, okay, it did. After that weekend it was easier and even more exciting to invite people to our church than ever? Not just because this man had helped me get my life back on track with the Lord. Not just because this man was leading a church that only three years earlier had about forty-five people attending on Sunday mornings and now over three times that many. Not just a man who was doing everything he could in his ministry to bring people to the Lord. But because he did all these things and many more by being real. Pastor Dave loves the Lord and you can tell it just by being around him. Not just by what he says but what he does. I had always thought of pastors walking around in suits all day long, always studying the word of God all day or in prayer to God all day. Never being wrong about anything in life. Always knowing the right answer for everything. They were on a pedestal above everyone else.

Pastor Dave burst that bubble for me. He showed me that not only did he wear suits, study his Bible, and pray to God, and answer important biblical questions for people, he did not do it 24/7. He was available if need be, but sometimes even though he is Pastor Dave he is also just Dave. Dave liked camping, he liked boating, and he liked cooking on an open fire. But he did it in a way that was pleasing to the Lord. That made me feel better since I was going to be filling in for him in just a few short weeks.

Now the last time I had preached in front of a church body there were about seventy people present. On an average we had about one hundred seventy-five people coming to church on Sunday mornings at First Baptist. I love to talk; ask anybody who knows me, they will tell you. I love talking about the Lord or the Bible in general, Bible stories. But I would rather talk one on one or to a small group. In large groups I get a little nervous. But when given the opportunity I do it because I believe that's what God would have me to do. And in doing so I look for two things to help me through such times. First from the Bible, In 1 Corinthians 2:1-5 it says, "When I came to you, brothers, I did not come with eloquence or superior wisdom as I proclaimed to you the testimony about God. For I resolved to know nothing while I was with you except Jesus Christ and him crucified. I came to you in weakness and fear, and with much trembling. My message and my preaching were not with wise and persuasive words, but with a demonstration of the Spirit's power, so that your faith might not rest on men's wisdom, but on God's power."

When I stand up in front of a large group of people and share things about God with them, I cannot do it on my own. I would be a wreck. I leave it up to the Holy Spirit working through me to do it for me. Now I have to take the time to prepare the message but I cannot do it on my own. But when I read that the apostle Paul, who wrote at least thirteen of the New Testament books, had the same problem as I do when speaking to large groups of people, that gives me courage to do it myself.

The second thing that helps me is knowing that Pastor Dave used to get so upset before preaching his sermons, that he would actually throw up. Now this is a man that at a drop of a hat I have seen speak in front of people without anything prepared ahead of time. So that gives me the courage to keep getting up in front of groups of people, small or large, and doing the best I can for the Lord. A line from an old hymn we sang as youngsters is "Do then the best you can, not for rewards, not for the praise of man but for the Lord."

I went to work and immediately began telling co-workers that I was going to be preaching on Father's Day at my church. They would look at me and say, "Why? What are you doing that for? How come? Are you nervous?" So I would tell them my pastor was going on vacation and just asked if I would fill in for him, and no, I was not nervous, not yet anyway.

The day after our camping trip I began a journey that was a trial in itself. I spent the first week praying and reading my Bible as usual, trying to find the subject for my sermon. Trying to come up with something with a Father's Day theme. That just did not pan out for me. Father's Day theme just wasn't working for me at all. So I continued praying and searching the Bible for my sermon subject. Diana would ask me, "How's it going? Know what your sermon is going to be about yet?"

"Nope," I would tell her, "not yet, still looking."

By the beginning of the third week I had come up with either the Fruit of the Spirit or maybe the True Vine as my subject. But I just wasn't feeling it. Those subjects, as good as they are, just weren't stirring up my spirit like I felt they should be. Usually I get very excited about my sermon subjects and it just wasn't happening this go-round. I continued praying about it but I felt hopeless. Deep in my spirit I felt like I really just wanted to tell people how God was working in my life, how God had brought me back from the dead so to speak. My own personal testimony about everything God had been doing since I had came back home to him and to the church. But I really did not think anyone cared about my story. Who would want to hear about how God was working mighty things in my life. That would just sound like I was bragging or, it was probably just pride trying to edge its way into my life. I didn't want anything to do with pride, so I forgot about it and continued struggling looking for the perfect sermon. Wednesday night at praise practice, Pastor Dave asked me, "Well, Kermit, what are you preaching on? What's the topic for Sunday?"

I said, "Well, I'm not sure yet."

If you could have seen his face! He rolled his eyes a little, but he didn't say anything. But I thought to myself, *He probably thinks I left this man in charge giving spiritual guidance of some sort to the congregation on Sunday and he's not sure what his topic is. Oh, brother!*

But I quickly gave him some hope something to cling to. I told him I was thinking about preaching on the Fruit of the Spirit, or the True Vine. Pastor Dave said, "John, chapter 15, Jesus the true vine, good," as he seemed somewhat relieved.

Thursday morning I woke up earlier than normal and was thinking about Philippians 4:7, "And the peace of God, which transcends all understanding, will guard your hearts and your minds in Christ Jesus." I thought to myself, Okay peace of God, peace, that's one of the fruits of the Spirit, that's a confirmation for the sermon topic Fruit of the Spirit. All right now I'm getting somewhere.

Thursday evening Diana asked me, "How's the message coming along?"

I told her I still wasn't sure about the scriptures I was planning on using. I still wasn't sure about the subject even though I had things rolling at this point finally.

Diana reminded me that people from our church and our family were praying for me. She said, "Don't worry, God will make it real to you tomorrow."

The next day was Friday. I had made plans to spend the entire day at a local campground working on the sermon. I took our camper down Thursday evening and set it up. All I had to do was get up Friday morning, get in my truck, drive three miles to the campground and spend the day working on the sermon. Diana was going to work Friday and then join me that evening at the campground. We would then spend the rest of the weekend just camping like we usually did.

Friday morning came. Diana and I got up and began getting ready for our day. Diana got ready for work, and I collected things I would be taking with me to the camper. A couple of versions of the Bible, a Bible dictionary, a concordance, a couple of notebooks for writing on and a couple of pens. I kissed Diana goodbye and headed for the campground.

I was still uneasy about my sermon so as I drove I began to pour out my heart to the Lord. About three-quarters of the way there the Lord said to me, **"If you tell them, they will listen."**

I asked, "If I tell them what Lord?"

"If you tell them the changes I have made in you since you have come back to me, they will listen," said the Lord. After hearing that I remembered I had shared at a men's group just one of the things God had done in my life since returning to the church and my relationship with the Lord. Some of them said, "Now, that's something the church needs to hear."

So I said, "Okay Lord," and pulled into camp relieved and ready to get started. I said another prayer asking the Holy Spirit to guide me, to help me remember everything God had done since my return to him and the church. I opened up my notebook and began writing.

Before I knew it the day had passed by, I had written about twenty pages in my notebook.

When Diana got there about 6:00 that evening. I was so excited I could hardly stand it. I began to tell her what had happened on the way over to the campground. How God had spoken to me and answered my prayer. I showed her the papers I had been writing all day. I was so into writing that day, I had not even started a fire to cook anything. So I whipped up a sandwich and cooked a package of flavored rice on the stove in the camper. I ate really fast and was back to writing again. I had begun rewriting my papers over again trying to make it sound more like a sermon instead of a story. I did start a fire and I sat at the picnic table while Diana sat by the fire.

Diana was so glad God had answered our prayers about the sermon, but she was feeling a little neglected at that moment. She had worked all day and was looking forward to spending the evening with me around the campfire, talking as we usually did on our camping trips. But I was totally captivated by what I was writing. Diana shared how she felt about the evening and I just told her I was sorry for not spending time with her. That God was depending on me to do my best on Sunday. Diana agreed and began reading the papers I was writing and commenting on them. After a while I did put the papers down and we spent the rest of the evening together around the fire talking about my sermon.

The next morning we woke up at camp and began our day with a nice walk around the campground and then breakfast. Diana took a ride home to take care of our dogs and I began working on my sermon once more. By the afternoon Diana and I realized there is no way I could tell everything I had written down in thirty or even forty-five minutes. So I sat down and on one side of my notebook wrote all my scriptures I wanted to use. 2 Chronicles 7:14, Romans 12:2, Galatians 5:22-23, Philippians 4:13, 1 John 4:4, and Hebrews 10:25.

On the other side of the notebook I wrote Title: Turning Tragedies into Victories. Talk about not going to church, talk about Mother's memorial service, talk about coming to First Baptist Church, talk about getting back into the Word, talk about family and friends who are now coming to church with us, talk about surrendering to God, talk about stop chewing tobacco, talk about lock-in. I told Diana since she would be sitting up front to nod at me when I had ten minutes left and I would know it was time to wrap it up.

This sermon for me was the best I had ever given, I thought, for a couple of reasons. First it was the first time I did not basically read my entire sermon from my notebook. That's why I just wrote lines of what I was going to talk about. It had to come from the heart and from the power of the Holy Spirit if I was to get through the sermon. Not relying on my paper but trusting in the Lord to see me through the sermon. That sermon was full of personal emotions. That day the people in the congregation laughed with me and cried with me. There were a couple of times where I had to pause for a moment and collect my thoughts and emotions, but God helped me through those moments.

When I was done with my sermon that day, I had not told all God had done for me in those last eighteen months, but I said enough that the people sitting in those pews that day heard how God loves us unconditionally. That he is always there for us. James 4:8 says, "Come near to God and he will come near to you."

When I finished that message that day I felt as close to God then as I had ever felt before. I had trusted totally in the power of the Holy Spirit that lives in me and works through me that day. Practically the whole church either shook my hand, or was hugging my wife and me, telling us how glad they were I had shared my testimony with them. That day the spoken words God had given to me a couple of days earlier came to pass. "*If you tell them, they will*

listen." I received my resurrection miracle promise from Easter on Father's Day. God through Pastor Dave had given me a chance to preach again, something I had not done for over ten years.

A good friend and co-worker of mine Darin, came and brought his family to church that Sunday morning to hear me preach. At work on Monday Darin told me, "Well, that wasn't what I expected. It was more of a personal testimony than a sermon."

I told him yes he was right but that's what God wanted me to share with the congregation. He said, "You know, my daughter Lacey said to me, 'Dad, Kermit made me cry.' He said, "I told her that's okay, he made me cry too."

Chapter Eight

*N*ot long after that I was having trouble listening to my music and Bible CDs at work. It was just so loud in the area where I worked, it was hard for me to hear them any longer. Frustrated and starting to get upset when I could not hear the CDs, I just began to tell God, "I need help here. All I want to do is come to work do my job and worship you while I work."

After a couple of weeks I was moved from the area in the plant where I had been working for almost twenty years, to a different part of the plant doing the same type of work, just in a different area. The area was over in a corner of the plant away from everyone working on the production lines so it was not as noisy. Plus the person I worked next to, Don, was someone who did not mind listening to the Christian music or the Bible because he also is a Christian. God had answered my prayer. Thank you, Father.

I was so excited to be able to listen to the music and the scriptures again I could hardly stand it. Don was enjoying it also. We would listen to the Bible and then discuss what we thought it meant.

Malachi 3:16 says, "Then those who feared the Lord talked with each other, and the Lord listened and heard." Isn't that cool? Every time we talk about the Lord with another believer God listens and hears what we are saying about him. Then through the power of the Holy Spirit he can guide our hearts and minds toward him as we open up more and more to his calling upon our lives.

But after a few weeks Don was moved and I was left there with only one other person in my work area, Theresa. As I listened to the word every day I began to share with her things from the Bible I heard that day or things that had happened in my life. She seemed interested in my conversations so I would share with her from time to time. Then we became a little busier and another co-worker, Nina, was moved into my work area. Nina worked right next to me so I would try not to turn the CDs up too loud. But she told me that was okay, it wasn't bothering her. Every now and then she would ask me to stop the CD and she would ask me a question about what she had heard or she would comment on it. Now the three of us in that area began sharing with each other things about our lives, about our thoughts on God, the Bible, and about church.

About this time I had saw a TV program about camping that had a segment on it about teardrop campers. Teardrop campers began around the late thirties, early forties, for two people to camp in. They are typically 4 feet wide, 4 feet high and 8 feet long. The front part you sleep in and the back opens up into a galley or kitchen area where you store food and water and other stuff. I had watched this same TV program three years earlier and saw those teardrop campers and wanted to build one. But I talked myself out of it because I did not think I could build one that would be nice enough to actually take camping. And when I first told some of my co-workers about building one they just rolled their eyes at me. One of them said, "What kind of a hillbilly camper would that be? You already have a big camper. Why would you want to camp in that little thing?" But one weekend sitting at the campground I took out a notebook and began drawing up a diagram of a teardrop. Even Diana thought I was a little nuts, but she is used to me by now. We had been married for fifteen years at that point.

A couple of weeks later I began my project. First I built a model of my diagram. It was 18 inches wide, 18 inches high and 3 feet long. We were camping with Pastor Dave and his family again. So I told him about the teardrop camper I wanted to build. When we went home to feed our dogs, I picked up the model to show him. He seemed to like the idea, thought it was cool looking, but I think he was a little puzzled about why I would give up staying in our 24 ft. camper to stay in that little camper.

A week or so after that I started building the camper. I learned a great deal about teardrops, from the best camping message board forum (in my opinion) on the net, Teardrops & Tiny Travel Trailers. You can find a lot of information on that board and the people are friendly. As the teardrop began to take shape, Diana began to have a little more interest in it. She would come out to the garage and see if I needed help in the evenings. My neighbors would come over and look at it. Actually, I would almost drag them over to see it. Then they would help now and then if I asked them for help.

Pastor Dave called me one day and asked if I had found windows for my teardrop camper. I told him no, and he told me he had bought me two windows at a flea market, if I wanted them. He thought they would work. I hung up the phone and went right over; they would work great for the camper.

I took lots of pictures during the building of our teardrop camper, which are on the camping forum. The more I worked on it the more I liked it and the more excited I was that I had decided to build it. One month and 119 hours of labor later it was finished. We took it camping the very day I finished working on it. Not only was I proud of it, but also Diana, and our neighbors.

I took my pictures to work and showed my co-workers. They seemed to be impressed on my accomplishment too. It did not look like a hillbilly camper after all. After taking the time to build that little camper and how proud I was of how well it turned out, I shared with the praise and worship team at one of our meetings how I thought God must feel about us when we do things that make him proud of us. I molded and build that little camper into what I had imagined in my mind it should look like when I was finished with it. God has in mind what he wants us to be like when he is finished with us. Sometimes we are molded in ways that we don't understand, ways that even hurts at times in our lives. But God our master builder knows what is best for us as he molds us into the clay vessel he wants us to be, if we let him.

By the time I was forty-eight God was continually working amazing things in my life. Our Sunday school class or small group were becoming closer and closer with one another. Each week we would just read the word of God and discuss it with each other and share personal experiences in our lives. On one particular night Diana was awakened during the night and one of our group members was on her mind. She began to pray for him, not knowing what for or why but the Holy Spirit prompted her to pray, so she did. When we got to praise practice the next day Pastor Dave told us that Don, one of our Sunday school members, was in the hospital and that we needed to pray for him, that his heart was not doing very well. He'd had a heart attack a few years earlier and it had left his heart with only about a third of it functioning. But the night before he had an attack at home and was not doing very well at all. We held him up in prayer that night. Diana and I prayed for him at home the rest of the week.

Testify

On Sunday morning, Don was at church. God had touched him and restored the majority of his heart back to working correctly. That morning during our Sunday school class Don told us what had happened. Diana told him earlier in the week she was awoken up in the night and he was on her mind. Don told her, "That was when I was having my attack, the time you were awakened."

Isn't God amazing? Could God have healed Don without Diana praying for him? Without the church praying for him? Of course he could. But he chooses to show us again and again that he is real, that he is not a figment of our imagination. That he can and will prove to us that he is who he says he is, that he can do what he says he can do any time he wishes to. It's amazing. God will just take scripture and make it come alive to us.

Three mornings in a row I woke up thinking about Ezekiel, The Valley of Dry Bones. Beginning from the first morning I would read it from the word of God. The next morning I would wake up thinking about it again and read it once again. Finally on the third day I said, "Lord, what are you trying to tell me with these verses from Ezekiel chapter 37?" God was speaking a prophecy through Ezekiel for Israel. But that prophecy was not only about Israel but about my life and the life of the church. Not just my local church I was attending but the whole body of Christ. The Spiritual Church. It's time not only for me but the entire body of Christ to start doing the things God has called us to do. It time for me and the Church to put our eyes on Jesus and do the things he told us to do. It's time for me and the Church to think about our eternal destiny and not just where we are today.

What has God called us to do? Matthew 28:18-20 says, "Then Jesus came to them and said, "All authority in heaven and on earth has been given to me. Therefore go and make disciples of all nations, baptizing them in the name of the Father and of the Son and of the Holy Spirit, and teaching them to obey everything I have commanded you. And surely I am with you always, to the very end of the age." We are to make disciples. We are seeing a lot of people getting saved and that's great but Jesus said we need to make disciples out of them.

John 14:23-24 says, "Jesus replied, if anyone loves me, he will obey my teaching. My Father will love him, and we will come to him and make our home with him. He who does not love me will not obey my teaching. These words you hear are not my own; they belong to the Father who sent me." Jesus taught us many things from his word that we need to be doing better: helping the poor, feeding the hungry, visiting the sick, just to name a few. Jesus said if we love him we will do these things.

Jesus speaking in Matthew 6:19-21, "Do not store up for yourselves treasures on earth, where moth and rust destroys, and where thieves break in and steal. But store up for yourselves treasures in heaven, where moth and rust do not destroy, and where thieves do not break in and steal. For where your treasure is, there your heart will be also." We live in a materialistic world; there is no denying that fact. And there is nothing wrong with having material things as long as they do not hold on to our hearts. Our greatest treasure we have needs to be our personal relationship with our creator, our savior, and our teacher, God.

So I began to try and improve on these matters in my life, and try to make other brothers and sisters in Christ aware of these same issues. I began sharing more at work with Theresa and Nina. They said they liked it when I shared with them about my faith. They may not always agree with me on everything I say but they were willing to listen just the same. And it means a lot to me that at least they are willing to listen.

As I continue in God's word he reveals new things to me every day. If you read the Bible once in your lifetime you're only going to understand it from your first observation of it. The more and more you read the word of God the more the Holy Spirit opens up your mind and your thoughts to better understand what you are reading. The Bible does not change, but as you become more and more acquainted with the word you just get a better understanding of what different things in the word means to you. As you mature as a Christian, the Holy Spirit reveals new things to you. Here is just one example of what I am saying. Jesus tells us in Luke16:19-31, about the rich man and Lazarus. "There was a rich man who was dressed in purple and fine linen and lived in luxury every day. At his gate was laid a beggar named Lazarus, covered with sores. And longing to eat what fell from the rich man's table. Even the dogs came and licked his sores. The time came when the beggar died and the angels carried him to Abraham's side. The rich man also died and was buried. In hell, where he was in torment, he looked up and saw Abraham far away, with Lazarus by his side. So he called to him, 'Father Abraham, have pity on me and send Lazarus to dip the tip of his finger in water and cool my tongue, because I am in agony in this fire.'

But Abraham replied, 'Son, remember that in your lifetime you received your good things, while Lazarus received bad things, but now he is comforted here and you are in agony. And besides all this between us and you a great chasm has been fixed, so that those who want to go from here to you cannot, nor can anyone cross over from there to us.'

He answered, 'Then I beg you, father, send Lazarus to my father's house, for I have five brothers. Let him warn them, so that they will not also come to this place of torment.'

Abraham replied, 'They have Moses and the Prophets; let them listen to them.'

'No, Father Abraham,' he said, 'but if someone from the dead goes to them, they will repent.'

He said to him, 'If they do not listen to Moses and the Prophets, they will not be convinced even if someone rises from the dead."

I have heard this story from the Bible read to me by preachers many times, I have read commentaries on this story from the Bible a few times, and I have personally read this story from the Bible many times. There are a lot of things we can learn from this famous Bible story. But in all my years of hearing and reading this story, not until I was forty-seven years of age did I realize the main point of the story. The whole story your mind is focused on the rich man in torment, and Lazarus is by Abraham's side. The rich man asks if Lazarus could help him, and is told he could not. Then he asked if Lazarus could go and warn his family. Again he is told no, they have Moses and the Prophets to listen to. The rich man says if someone from the dead goes they will listen.

Your mind is totally focused on those two men that have died. But here is the surprise: Verse 31 Jesus said they will not listen even if someone rises from the dead. Not if Lazarus but if someone. Jesus was predicting his own resurrection, not Lazarus. There were people there he talked to, that saw him heal people, that saw him do miracle after miracle and did not believe in him. And after he rose from the dead they still did not believe in him or who he was.

Reading the word of God is always an adventure to me. The Holy Spirit continually reveals new things to me as I read or listen to his word. Now I had been studying and thinking a lot about spiritual gifts. They are primarily written about in Romans, Chapter 12, and 1 Corinthians, Chapter 12. I had been studying these chapters of the Bible, and watching a DVD I had gotten from one of the TV preachers I watch. The DVD was about the spiritual gifts and the baptism of the Holy Spirit. That with the baptism of the Holy Spirit your Christian walk will be better, that the Holy Spirit will work his power through whoever is baptized in the Holy Spirit.

As I began reading more and more on the gifts and the baptism of the Holy Spirit, the more and more I wanted to be empowered to live this holy baptized life. I was on the internet checking out different articles on the Holy Spirit baptism and speaking in tongues. In one article it read. *Every person who has been baptized in the Holy Spirit will speak in tongues. Speaking in tongues is The Only Evidence of the baptism of the Holy Spirit. They go hand in hand as demonstrated in Acts 2:4.* Which reads, "All of them were filled with the Holy Spirit and began to speak in other tongues as the Spirit enabled them." The article on the internet said just open up your mouth and begin to speak. The Holy Spirit will put words in your mouth.

I tried this for two or three days and nothing happened except I would just sit there mumbling. No words came out of my mouth, no other language, and I began to get frustrated. I prayed *God, don't you want me to have the power I need to do the work you want me to do for you? Don't you want me to have the power to live the kind of Christian life you want me to live for you?* As I sat there upset because God was not allowing me to speak in tongues, I also began to think I was not worthy to be baptized in the Holy Spirit or worthy to be used by God to speak in tongues.

Then God spoke to me in the Spirit and said to me: "Stop asking me to baptize you in the Holy Spirit. You already are baptized in the Holy Spirit. And stop asking me for the gift of tongues. That gift is not for you. You already have your gifts from me. Use those gifts."

At that moment I remembered the Holy Spirit gives the gifts to whomever he wants to have them. That's part of the Holy Spirit's ministry to the believers in Christ, to give the gifts out as he determines in the body of Christ. 1 Corinthians 12:11 says, "All these are the work of one and the same Spirit, and he gives them to each one, just as he determines."

So I realized speaking in tongues was not "The Only Evidence" of being baptized in the Holy Spirit, only one of them. And that not everyone who is baptized with the Holy Spirit will speak in tongues, only the ones who God determines. That if you are walking in the power of the Spirit and using the gifts of the Spirit God has given you, that is your evidence of the baptism of the Holy Spirit. The gifts of the Holy Spirit are given to us for others, not just for us. We are to recognize our gifts and use them for others, not just for ourselves.

In January I went by the church to talk with Pastor Dave. I was filling him in on how my life was going, how God had been working in and through my life during that time. About the church, how it was growing, about his sermons, how they had changed my life that past year and how I was looking forward to the coming year.

As I was getting up to leave I remembered one more thing, though. I told Pastor Dave I really felt like he needed to speak on fasting one Sunday morning.

Pastor Dave said, "You know, I was going to tell you I am going to speak on that very thing this Sunday coming up. God has laid on my heart to fast for one week." Pastor Dave said he had already told some other people about it and was hoping I would join him and participate in the fast. Pastor Dave was going to speak on it Sunday morning and tell people they were welcome to join him if they would like to for one meal, one day, two days or all week, however the Spirit led them to fast.

So I told him, "Okay, I will join you in the fast." Now I had fasted many times in the past few years for one day, and what I mean by one day is actually just a couple of meals in a day. When I generally fast I skip breakfast, and take no food with me to work and eat nothing until I get home from work. Sometimes I have a snack after work or sometimes I will not eat until supper after Diana gets home from work around 5:30 in the evening. Diana and I will both fast at times usually on Wednesdays, or sometimes I will wake up and be led by the Holy Spirit to fast on any given day.

What was different about the week I talked to Pastor Dave was when we talked on Thursday, I had been led by the Holy Spirit to fast not only on Wednesday that week but also on Monday. That had been the first time I had ever fasted twice in one week. When I got home from the meeting that evening at supper I told Diana I was going to fast along with Pastor Dave for seven days, one whole week. Of course she thought we were a little nuts but said, "Okay, but I'm not going to fast for a week, maybe once or maybe twice for the day."

People fast in different ways these days. When I fast and the fast that Pastor Dave was speaking about was a fast of no food at all. We were going to drink water, fruit juices, milk, any kind of liquids, just no solid foods.

Fasting for me is a spiritual discipline. I believe that when you deny your body food, you are telling your physical body that the spiritual part of you is more important at that particular time in your life. You are saying to your natural body, the Holy Spirit and my spirit together are in control. Pastor Dave was looking for some guidance from God in his leading of the church in the coming year. I prayed for the Lord to give me guidance for my life for the year to come and beyond, guidance I could live my life by, as I began the fast that Sunday.

One of my prayers that day was that when I woke up in the mornings the following week, that God would reveal to me something he either wanted me to know or something he wanted me to do. Just have it on my mind when I woke up each morning. So Monday through Friday every morning I had some kind of a revelation from God. Monday was the only day I actually had two things that came to mind when I first woke up. The first one: the week before at our church a family had a baby die. I do not know in my spirit if I was questioning about that child's death or what. But my heavenly Father confirmed in me by the Holy Spirit that I could rest in the promises of God. The baby had not been left alone Angels had taken that child's spirit to be with Jesus in heaven. Thank you, Father. What a loving Father in heaven we have to love us enough to settle something I must have been struggling with in my spirit that I wasn't even aware of in my natural body!

The second one was Ezekiel, Chapter 47, so I got my Bible and began to read it. Verses 1-6 says, "The man brought me back to the entrance of the temple, and I saw water coming out from under the threshold of the temple toward the east (for the temple faced the east). The water was coming down from under the south side of the temple, south of the altar. He then brought me out through the north gate and led me around the outside to the outer gate facing east, and the water was flowing from the south side. As the man went eastward with a measuring line in his hand, he measured off a thousand cubits and then led me through water that was ankle-deep. He measured off another thousand cubits and led me through water that was knee-deep. He measured off another thousand and led me through water that was up to my waist. He measured off another thousand, but now it was a river that I could not cross, because the water had risen and was deep enough to swim in a river that no one could cross. He asked me, 'Son of man, do you see this?' Then he led me back to the bank of the river."

I read this passage from the Bible and meditated on it all that day, wondering what God was trying to tell me from those scripture verses. Before the day was over God revealed to me what I was to learn from those verses. The water flowing from the temple was the Holy Spirit. I was to lay myself down on the altar at the temple as a living sacrifice for God. As I left myself on the altar and walked away I needed to rely on the Holy Spirit more and more and myself less and less. The farther away from the altar, (myself) I got, the more and more the Holy Spirit will help my faith grow. The water not only represented the presence of the Holy Spirit but also the power of the Holy Spirit. The farther away from myself I got, the more power the Holy Spirit could work in me and through me to be a more effective witness for the Lord. Every day I need to ask God to fill me with the presence and the power of the Holy Spirit so that I might be a better witness for him each day in not only words but also deeds.

Tuesday morning I woke up and the Holy Spirit put on my mind to get a list of everyone who attended church and to pray for them. Diana called the church secretary and she left a list for me in my mail box at church. On Wednesday night we had praise practice so I picked up the list. I received a list of everyone who had been coming to church for the last two months. I first prayed over the entire list and then prayed specifically for everyone who had came to church in the last two months individually. Each day I would pray for several people until I finally finished the list. It took me a while but I got through it with the Holy Spirit's help.

Wednesday as I woke up the Holy Spirit brought to mind for me that on Sunday morning I was to go to church earlier than normal, go up to the prayer loft and pray. I was to pray for the Holy Spirits guidance that day for everyone at church, and then just pray as the Spirit led me. After I finished praying I was to go down into the sanctuary and walk by every pew and lay my hands on them. Now I thought to myself that last part of that request was kind of weird but I thought the Lord works in mysterious ways. So I told Diana that we had to go to church earlier than normal. She wanted to know why so I told her and she just said okay.

Sunday morning came. I went up to the prayer loft went into a closet and closed the door, got down on my knees and began praying. A few minutes later when I felt I was done I went down to the sanctuary and walked down the middle aisle and touched each pew as I walk by it. I turned around and did the same thing on the way back. I then went through the sound and computer area and made sure I touched each chair there also.

We went to our Sunday school class and then to the church service. Just before Pastor Dave finished he told everyone we would be having a special meeting right after church, for everyone to stick around if they would, and for those who were visiting to have a great day.

After a few minutes the meeting started. Pastor Dave gave a short talk on how the Spirit had led him, and some of the church leaders, to look for another staff member to help him with some of his duties because the church was growing to big for him alone. We watched a five minute video about a young man, his wife, four young children and one on the way. Then the church was asked if they had any questions and then we voted. All in favor say yes, "Yes," all opposed. Not one person in the entire church said no. Six months later this man and his family became a part of our church family.

I have said it before and I'm saying it again. We do not always understand why the Holy Spirit asks us to do things. We just need to trust the Lord and do them. God knows best.

Wednesday night I felt the Holy Spirit urging me to give to a certain ministry $84 a month this coming year. I also felt that was a lot of extra money to be giving away for the whole year. Thursday morning the Holy Spirit brought to mind the same figure and the same idea I had the night before. So I told Diana. She said it would make us stretch a little but okay, and I told her it had to be paid out of our first paycheck of the month every month. She agreed.

Friday morning was my last one for the week. The Holy Spirit must have thought my plate was full enough. But Friday morning the Holy Spirit reminded me of a sermon I had preached several years earlier. "Seek ye first the Kingdom of God." I found my notebook with that sermon in it. I read it and thought about it all day, Friday and Saturday. Afterwards I realized that there is nothing in this life more important than Seeking God First in all that we do. And just like that before I knew it my week of fasting was over and I had made it.

Diana felt bad the first few days eating without me but I told her, "Do not feel guilty on my account. I choose to fast for a week, not you."

And how did I do it? Actually it was simple. The Holy Spirit helped me through the use of God's word. Once again I drew upon Jesus' temptation as my example. In Matthew 4:1-4, "Then Jesus was led by the Spirit into the desert to be tempted by the devil. After fasting forty days and forty nights, he was hungry. The tempter came to him and said, "If you are the Son of God; tell these stones to become bread." Jesus answered, "It is written: Man does not live on bread alone, but on every word that comes from the mouth of God."

Every time I felt tempted to eat I would just say to myself. Man does not live on bread alone but by every word that comes from God. And the urge would go away just like it did when I stopped chewing tobacco by quoting scripture. There were a few challenges besides just hunger that week. Seemed like every day someone brought something to work and tried to get me to eat. They did not know I was fasting all week, they were just being their normal selves. We were treated at work with pizza and pop that week, just my luck, that only happens a couple times a year but I did not give in.

Come Sunday after church I was ready to eat, but I tried not to overdo it since I hadn't eaten in a week. The family wanted to go to a buffet after church but I only had one plate of food; my stomach had shrunk from not eating. And it's not the reason to fast, but I also had lost fifteen pounds that week.

The following week the Christian TV channel I watch, Cornerstone, was having one of their telethons to raise money for their station. I felt the Holy Spirit urging me to give them $30 a month. Once again I told Diana. She said yes but that it would really be stretching us. We were already going to be giving to the other ministry $84 a month.

I prayed and said, "Lord, I believe you want me to give this money to these two ministries but it is going to stretch us financially. Your word says in Deuteronomy 8:18, "But remember the Lord your God, for it is he who gives you the ability to produce wealth." Lord I need you to help me make this extra money you are asking us to give this next year. I'm putting my trust in you to provide me with the extra income. And I will pay these the first of every month."

I told Diana to make sure those two payments go out with the first paycheck of each month. We were faithful with paying to these ministries and God was faithful in providing me with the power to produce extra wealth at my work. I worked an abundant amount of overtime on my job. We not only had enough to pay those extra two ministries but we gave money to others also that year as the Holy Spirit led us. Thank you heavenly Father.

A couple of weeks after the fast was over my fellow Christian brother and co-worker Hook was sick with a cold again. It seemed like he was getting a cold every time he turned around. One day in a moment of weakness I thought to myself, *Hook sure is getting sick a lot. Maybe if he had fasted a week like I did he wouldn't be getting sick so much.* That's all it took. One small letting down of my guard and pride marched right in. A couple of days after that I caught the worst cold I have had in years. I had that cold for over a week. Pride was Satan's downfall. I did not want it to continue in me so I asked God to forgive me for thinking such prideful things. We need to keep ourselves humbled or God may humble us instead. I think the former is better than the latter.

Hebrews 12:5-6 says, "And you have forgotten that word of encouragement that addresses you as sons: My son do not make light of the Lord's discipline, and do not lose heart when he rebukes you, because the Lord disciplines those he loves, and he punishes everyone he accepts as a son."

Believe it or not, these words still ring true today. God still disciplines his children. We do not hear this message much today. It's not one of the popular subjects of the day. We would rather hear how much God is love and how much God loves us. And he does. That's why he disciplines us, because he loves us so much and wants the very best for us.

It goes on in Hebrews 12:7-11, "Endure hardship as discipline; God is treating you as sons. For what son is not disciplined by his father? If you are not disciplined (and everyone undergoes discipline) then you are illegitimate children and not true sons. Moreover, we have all had human fathers who disciplined us and we respected them for it. How much more should we submit to the Father of our spirits and live! Our fathers disciplined us for a little while as they thought best; but God disciplines us for our good, that we may share in his holiness. No discipline seems pleasant at the time, but painful. Later on, however, it produces a harvest of righteousness and peace for those who have been trained by it."

Jesus speaking in Matthew 23:12, "For whoever exalts himself will be humbled, and whoever humbles himself will be exalted." When we realize we are exalting ourselves in prideful thoughts or words, we need to humble ourselves to God ask for forgiveness and God will lift us up.

Chapter Nine

*A*s time went by I continued to listen to Christian music and the Bible on CD at work, and I was still sharing from time to time with my co-workers. But mostly I tried to set before them a good example of the Christian walk. I was still watching Christian TV primarily to help keep my mind focused on Godly things. I was watching a program and the host of the show was talking to an author about a book he had written. In this book he talked about a time line in our lives and how God has a destiny for each one of us. How that time line will help you see and discover your own destiny. It was so interesting that I sat down and began writing about my life, my time line, trying to see if I had a destiny I could discover.

Ten pages later I was amazed at what I discovered. On my road I noticed how God was so much a part of my life and the road I had walked. Many times I turned off the main road onto side roads but somehow God had gotten me back on the main road, back on track.

Jesus in Matthew 7:13-14, "Enter through the narrow gate. For wide is the gate and broad is the road that leads to destruction, and many enter through it. But small is the gate and narrow the road that leads to life, and only a few find it." God throughout my life had helped me walk that narrow road and with his help I hope to continue to walk it.

As I thought about how God had been such an influence in my life I wondered if anyone would be interested in reading about my life. How so many times in my life God had intervened and helped me. How so many times I had failed God but he forgave me. How many times he had worked miracles in my life. As I pondered all these things I felt like God wanted me to write them in a book. That God wanted me to share my life with others, to show how God can change people's lives if we let him. At first I thought no one cares to know about my life. Who would want to read about me? I am nobody famous, I'm just a factory worker trying to live a life for the Lord the best way I can. I'm just an ordinary man. But God showed me that the people he used in the Bible were all just ordinary people except for one, his only begotten son Jesus Christ. His very own apostles whom he choose were fishermen, a tax collector, and one was a former zealot, a political radical. I prayed about it and felt confident God wanted me to write a book about my life. I told Diana and by this time in our lives she just said whatever you think God wants you to do, just do it. I shared my idea with our neighbors Keith and Helen whom we spend a lot of time with. They seemed to like the idea somewhat. I have already shared most of my life with them, being neighbors for the past twenty years. I really did not think I would have enough for a book more like a pamphlet but I began writing it anyway. I went to the book store at our local mall and realized all books don't have to be hundreds of pages in length. There were some that had only a few short pages. Then I felt a little more encouraged about the book. My neighbor, Helen then told me she had a dream my book was published. That gave me a little more hope.

As I wrote God would just bring into my memory all kinds of things that happened throughout my life. I took the first page to church and shared it with my Sunday school class and they seemed to enjoy it. Connie asked, "What are you planning on doing with that?"

I told her, "Hopefully write enough for a book, get it published to help others come to know God through his son, Jesus."

After about the first ten pages I printed it off and let Keith and Helen read it. Helen likes to read so I thought I would get some feedback from her and her husband. They both seemed to like it. Next I gave it to two of my co-workers, Theresa and Nina. They took it home and read it. They gave me a good report also and by then I was really getting excited about my book. I asked them if they thought it was interesting enough to read a whole book about. If they thought my stories were interesting enough? They both said they liked hearing me talk about my life and my faith. That was encouraging also.

After about two months of writing in my spare time I had about twenty or twenty-five pages written. I printed them off and took them to church. One of my Christian brothers at church had just graduated college. I wanted his opinion on my book as a college graduate. I wondered if he would be interested in reading more of my book. If he thought the story moved along well enough, did I have enough scripture, too many scriptures? Those kind of questions.

I could hardly wait until Wednesdays praise practice to see what he thought. Wednesday came and I asked him, "Well, what did you think? Don't just be nice. I want the truth."

He said he liked it very much. That he would not change anything in his opinion. Keep writing it the same way. There was only one thing he noticed. He said, "You have a lot of misspelled words. Do you want me to correct them for you?"

I laughed. I told him I was sorry spelling is not one of my strong points. But that was okay. Diana was going to correct my spelling for me. So I pressed on with the book writing every chance I got. I would sit down to write and God would just bring to my mind something that had happened in my life.

By this time it was camping season again. We went with Pastor Dave's brother Brian and his family the first weekend out. We love going camping with them. Brian works for the state park and he loves to walk. On a weekend camping with them we will walk in the park at least a half a dozen times. We share meals together, we share our life stories together. We talk about church, we talk about the Bible, and we sing songs together.

A few short weeks later we were camping together again. Brian brought along his keyboard and we were trying to put music to a couple of songs I had written. After messing around with that for a while Brian pulled out the sheet music for songs we sing on the praise and worship team at church. We sang *In the Secret, How Great is our God,* and a few others. We were camped across the road and down a couple of camp sites from the camp store. As we began to sing we noticed that a small crowd had begun to form at the store. They would go into the store buy something, come out of the store, stand there and listen to us sing. We are not professional by any means but the people just seemed to be drawn to the music. Finally we sang all the ones we liked from the music Brian had and stopped singing. Some of the people actually came by and thanked us for singing for them. How awesome it is that we were just singing songs we love from church worshiping God in our own little way while camping and people were blessed by it. God uses us at any given moment when we give him the opportunity.

The camp Chaplain asked us if we could come and sing at the camp service on Sunday but we were singing at our church on Sunday so we had to decline. But we said maybe later on in the summer, maybe we could when it wasn't our turn at church. She said ok and took Brian's phone number. We also camped with another couple from church, Robb, Barbara, and their daughter Hannah that summer. They had bought an old Airstream camper and we camped with them one weekend across from the camp store. We were asked at the camp store if we were going to sing again. I told them not this weekend; we were camping with another couple and no one brought a keyboard.

I love camping and the outdoors. Sometimes I think about the disciples sitting around the campfire listening to Jesus, the son of God and all his wisdom. Or maybe sitting down by the lake, or rides they took in boats across the lake.

In Matthew 13:1-9, Jesus tells us The Parable of the Sower. "That same day Jesus went out of the house and sat by the lake. Such large crowds gathered around him that he got into a boat and sat in it, while all the people stood on the shore. Then he told them many things in parables, saying: A farmer went out to sow his seed. As he was scattering the seed, some fell along the path, and the birds came and ate it up. Some fell on rocky places, where it did not have much soil. It sprang up quickly, because the soil was shallow. But when the sun came up, the plants were scorched, and they withered because they had no root. Other seed fell among thorns, which grew up and choked the plants. Still other seed fell on good soil, where it produced a crop a hundred, sixty or thirty times what was sown. He who has ears let him hear."

Jesus got into a boat by the lake and began to tell a parable to all the people who had gathered around him. A parable is an earthly story with a heavenly meaning. These parables that Jesus taught were wonderful stories. They make you use your mind and digest what Jesus has said. In the gospels of Matthew and Luke there are about thirty-eight parables that Jesus taught. Most of the parables, though, Jesus leaves for us to study and to meditate on to search out for the truths that are hidden within them. For a few of the parables, though, Jesus gives an explanation. But even those we still need to meditate upon them and the Holy Spirit will speak to us through them.

So in Matthew 13:18-23, Jesus gives us the answer to this parable. "Listen then to what the parable of the sower means: When anyone hears the message about the kingdom and does not understand it, the evil one comes and snatches away what was sown in his heart. This is the seed sown along the path. The one who received the seed that fell on rocky places is the man who hears the word and at once receives it with joy. But since he has no root, he last only a short time. When trouble or persecution comes because of the word, he quickly falls away. The one who received the seed that fell among the thorns is the man who hears the word, but the worries of this life and the deceitfulness of wealth choke it, making it unfruitful. But the one who received the seed that fell on good soil is the man who hears the word and understands it. He produces a crop, yielding a hundred, sixty or thirty times what was sown."

What an awesome story. This same parable is told in Luke 8:5-15. With the results being, the seed that is sown is the word of God. The different kinds of soils are people's hearts. And the hearts of mankind that take that seed, the word of God, water it with the Holy Spirit from God will produce a crop thirty, sixty, or one hundred times over.

This is evangelism at its best. As we begin to take God's word, believe it and apply it to our lives, as we begin to pray to God and ask for the Holy Spirit for guidance, as we begin to step out in faith and do the things God shows us in his word or ask us to do, we can see that crop begin to grow in others that we come in contact with. And God's word says if we apply these truths to our lives we will produce these multiple crops through our lives.

How is that possible? It's really simple if we think about it for a moment. If we just reach one person and lead him or her to Jesus, as they grow in the Lord they might lead one, two or even more to Jesus. We just have to trust God to help us plant the seed, the word of God in others. God has called each one of us, each one of his children to be sowers. Some of God's children are sowers to their spouses, some to their children, some to neighbors, some to co-workers, and some to strangers we don't even know. But sowers, we have been called to be. Some sowers will be writers, teachers, speakers, preachers, or maybe even TV evangelist. That's why I am writing this book. To sow the seed, God's word, into people's lives. Even if this book never gets published though I believe it will. Just writing my personal testimony down on paper, and letting others read it has already touched the lives of some who have read it. We have been called to sow God's word; God will water it through his Holy Spirit.

At work someone decided to put all the electric box builders in our building for the different assembly lines together in one area. So instead of just the three of us working in my area there were going to be five of us in one area. I wasn't sure if I liked the idea because of the close quarters I didn't know if I would be able to listen to my Christian music or my Bible CDs any longer.

Co-workers would come by and tell me just wait until the other two box builders begin working in this area you won't be able to hear your CDs any longer. They play country music on their radio and they play it loud. I would just say well we will just have to wait and see what happens then. I would just pray to God and tell him like before if he wanted me to listen to the Christian music and my Bible CDs he would have to intervene on my behalf.

The other two electric box builders moved into our work area, Bridget and Joyce, all of us felt like we were sardines in a can. But everyone kept their radios turned down to just loud enough for them to hear it in their own work area most of the time. There was a time of adjusting for all of us but as time went by we began to know more and more about each other. I began sharing with Bridget and Joyce about my life, some of my failures and some of my accomplishments. And I'm sure they were watching my actions as well as my words I spoke.

The year had been so busy I was working a lot of overtime. I had only five weeks in the last six months I hadn't worked any over time. I wasn't complaining God had blessed me with extra work since Diana and I were giving to those other two ministries on top of our regular giving to the Lord's work.

Even though we had been camping several times that summer it had not seemed like enough. The week of the Fourth of July we began our vacation. Starting the weekend before the Fourth of July and the weekend after the fourth we would have a total of nine days to go camping, yes. Time to be with Diana, time to share with each other in God's nature, the great outdoors. Time to reflect on our lives together and our lives with God Almighty. Life gets so busy at times we just have to stop and rest.

Our church was also very busy those days. We had been a part of the praise and worship team for two years. The church had continued growing in this time and we had switched from one service to two services on Sunday mornings. Not only that but we had started a children's church where they would not only learn Bible verses, have Bible studies, and fun games but also praise and worship. We had become very busy at church also. We were singing either for two church services or we were going to one church service and then singing praise and worship at the children's service. We enjoyed doing it, but we just needed a little rest.

I love camping also because we get away from the busyness of home life. We get in a rut at home, it seems at times. We seem to do the same things over and over and over. When camping Diana and I usually get some quality time with each other. We hold hands and take long walks together, actually having real conversations with each other, instead of the usual chitter-chatter at home.

We also enjoy meeting new people at the campgrounds or camping with friends. We planned on staying at one campground for three days moving to another one for three days and then finishing up at another one the last three days. Well, our original plans got messed up from the start of our vacation. We only stayed one night at our first stop because the state parks closed because of a budget problem. So we moved to another park, another state. Which wasn't that bad it was only ten miles from where we had been staying? Plus that's where we were planning on moving to anyway just a couple of days earlier.

We spent the next five days at that park and had a wonderful time. It only rained one out of the nine days of camping and it was a short-lived rain at that. We met an older couple staying in an old 15 ft. Scotty camper. The husband would sit around the campfire playing a harmonica while his wife would do word puzzles. He would go fishing and she would take naps. They enjoyed camping as much as we did.

We had sold our 24 ft. camper in the spring and bought a 13 ft. camper. People were stopping by wanting to look inside every now and then. A couple of days later people in the site next to us pulled in and set up camp in a 45 ft. motor coach. One afternoon we returned to camp from going and checking on our dogs at home. We saw the people in the motor coach trying to start a fire. They were not having a very successful time of it so I took over some wood out of the back of my truck, some good old dry wood that I knew would burn quite nice. We talked for a while and I told them they could help themselves to my wood I had plenty. They said, "Thanks." Diana and I went back to our campsite. The next day we did some running around. We were checking out other campgrounds to see where we might be staying the last couple of days. My pal, Brian, and his family were going to be joining us. We did not want to go too much farther away than we already were. One of our dogs at home was getting older and had not been feeling well.

As we made it back to camp, the sun was already beginning to go down. The people in the motor coach came right over and started taking wood out of my truck. The husband said, "I thought we were not going to have a fire tonight since you were not here." I just laughed as they grabbed an arm load of wood and headed to their camp site. I started our fire and we spent the rest of the night watching the flames of the fire and nodding.

Well, after some debate we decided to go to a campground only two miles down the road from where we were. All three campgrounds were around the same lake, all within ten miles of each other but in two different states. Friday we packed up, hooked up and moved to our final destination before going back home on Sunday.

The last time we'd camped with Brian and his family, his wife Connie had to work until 7:00 that evening so she just brought pizza to camp with her. Since we only moved a couple of miles from our last campsite I decided to make supper and have it ready when they arrived. But when Brian pulled up to set up camp, Connie and their daughter, Corrina, were with him. They got their camp set up and I surprised them with supper already cooked. We had dinner together and then it was walking time. We walked around the park and looked at other campers. Looking to see if we could find something different or unique. A short time after arriving back at camp Brian, Corrina, and I headed for the volleyball and basketball courts. We played around for about an hour and a half, then headed back to camp for the evening. Spent the rest of the evening sitting around the campfire and talking.

The next day we spent doing our camping things together. We went for walks, went swimming in the pool, and ate a lot of food. Since I had made supper Friday night, Connie made one of her great meals on Saturday for us to share. Sunday we had brunch together, fellowshipped together, packed up and headed for home. Nine wonderful days of camping had come to an end. They had been looked forward to and enjoyed to the fullest. We arrived home and began the task of unloading the camper. After that we sat down to relax before getting things ready for our return back to work on Monday morning.

The phone rang and it was our daughter Sarah. She had gone to church with our son Nicholas. Sarah was calling to let us know her grandparents were not at church that morning. Diana's mother and father had stayed home, and she wanted us to know so we could go by and check on them. They live only three miles away. Diana called first and her father answered the phone. Diana asked why they were not in church. Joe, her father said that Beva, Diana's mother, was still in bed sick. Diana asked what was wrong but he wasn't sure. We got in our car and headed over to check on Beva, Diana went to the bedroom and Beva wasn't really aware of her being there.

Diana called for an ambulance and called family members to let them know we were headed for the hospital. All of Beva's children and their spouses were with us and Joe at the hospital. After about five hours at our local hospital, the decision was made to fly Beva to an Erie hospital where her and Joe's heart doctor was. Joe rode with us as we all headed to Erie.

On the trip to Erie Joe said to us, "I hope Beva will be ok and by the way I have Alzheimer's."

Okay, we were not ready for that. "How come you or Mother haven't told us?" Diana asked.

"Well, we didn't want to worry you kids," Joe replied.

We all arrived about the same time around 11:30 p.m. We all met up together and waited to see what the doctor on call had to say to us. Finally the doctor came to speak with us. They were not sure what was wrong at that point but that Beva was very sick. We were told we could stay at the hospital and sleep in the waiting rooms if we wanted to. We all agreed to stay but we did not get much sleep that night. Everyone called off work and stayed together at the hospital.

The next day was more of the same. They kept trying to find out what exactly was wrong with Beva. We took Joe home, got cleaned up, grabbed his medicine and some clean clothes, and headed back to the hospital. Our son Nicholas and our daughter Sarah were going to take care of our dogs for us while we were in Erie.

We headed back to the hospital to find out nothing had really changed in Beva's condition. We spent another night at the hospital in the waiting room. On Tuesday morning the doctors finally figured out what was causing the problem. Beva had gall stones and the stones had caused infection in her blood and had shut down her kidneys. They put her on a kidney machine and tried to get her infection cleaned up. After that they were going to try and take the stone out.

We had all been taking turns going in and visiting with Beva and talking to her even though she was not coherent. Pastor Dave came and spent time with us and went in to see Beva. Before he left he prayed with us. That Tuesday evening Beva's health began to get worse. Around 10:30 p.m. Beva, Mom, at seventy-eight had taken her last breath.

Now we not only had to deal with the shock of losing Mom, we had to tell Joe and hope he didn't have another heart attack. The doctors took us in a room and explained everything to us and Joe. Joe had no physical problems with the news. We all decided to spend the night at the hospital instead of driving home upset.

I had not felt pain like what I was feeling at that moment since my mother had died 2 1/2 years earlier. I did not consider Beva to be my mother-in-law, just mother. She was someone you could always talk to about anything. She was always ready to give advice if called upon. Always ready to help in any way if at all possible. She loved everyone no matter who you were. But she had a special place in her heart set aside for her grandchildren and great grandchildren. Family meant everything to Beva and not just immediate family. She would welcome anyone into her family, especially other members of the family of God.

One example of what I mean is Hook, my co-worker, and his wife Anna. After they started coming to church with us they would occasionally go to lunch after church with us. Right away Beva began treating them like family. She did not really know them yet but she welcomed them into her family just like they were her own children. As time went on they began calling her Mom just like I did. That's what kind of an effect Beva had on people. If I had to describe Beva in one word that would be simple, Love. Being around Mom helped me to better understand God's love for mankind. Jesus was the greatest example of love for mankind but Beva, Mom to me, whom I could see in the flesh as an example, was number two. And following Jesus and knowing Mom has helped me to love in a much better way than I had ever loved before I knew her.

The next few days were hard on all of Beva's family. We couldn't leave Joe alone so different family members took turns staying with him. After Joe retired from the work force he had stopped driving.

Mom drove every where they went. She cooked, she washed the clothes, and she paid the bills. Mom just did everything for Joe. Now someone else was going to have to pick up where she left off. All of Beva's and Joe's children stuck together in helping him make decisions about the funeral. Everything from picking what funeral home to picking the casket to the funeral itself.

We met with Pastor Dave and made the same kind of decisions we had to make about my mother's memorial service. What kind of songs were her favorite, favorite Bible verses, hobbies she had. The family chose one viewing time. We thought it would be better for Joe because of his physical health and his age, eighty-three. The viewing was for three hours and there were people lined up to pay their respects. Afterwards we got time to say our last goodbyes to mom's body, but we look forward to the day when we will see her again in heaven.

The funeral was the next day at our church. Pastor Dave did the service and his brother, my camping buddy Brian, played the music. During the funeral the family members were asked if we had some thing we wanted to share about Beva. Pastor Dave knew I wanted to say something so he asked me to go first. With tears flowing down my cheeks I began talking.

I'm not sure of everything I said because it was so emotional, but I do remember saying that there were at least three things Beva and I shared. Our birthdays are on the same day, the love of her daughter Diana, and most of all the love we shared for God. On the morning of the funeral I had picked up Beva's Bible at her and Joe's home and was reading in it. I had noticed a poem she had saved from a newspaper clipping stuck in her Bible. I read it at her home and brought it with me to share with everyone there. With tears running down my face I read *Tomorrow Never Comes* by Norma Cornett Marek.

Chapter Ten

fter the funeral we had to figure out a schedule for taking care of Joe. We were all going to have to head back to work. We took turns going over every night and either cooking dinner for Joe or taking him out for dinner and spending time with him. All day long he was there by himself but we would spend the evenings with him. Pay his bills, wash his cloths, and just spend time with him. He was very lonely. Joe and Beva would have been married for sixty-one years a week after she died. So they were together a long time and he was lonely. After a couple of weeks the family tried to see if he would go to a personal care home but he wanted nothing to do with that idea. He thought we would put him in the home and never go see him.

So we decided it was best to let him stay at home. I would stop by on my way home from work to see if he needed anything and just to talk with him. Since he was there all day by himself, by the time I got there at 3:30 in the afternoon he was ready to talk. Diana and I told Pastor Dave we would have to step down from the praise and worship team for a while. Pastor Dave understood and told us to let him know when we were ready to join the team again and we said we would.

Since we had gone to two services we would have morning practice at 8:00 then first service started at 9:00. Joe did not want to go to church that early and sit there from 8:00 until 12:00 every Sunday. So we began picking him up for the second service every Sunday morning, and then all his children would meet for lunch after church. We would take Joe home afterwards and spend the afternoon with him together. While all this had been going on, Doug, our new executive minister had started working at the church. Also Phil, the college graduate who read the beginning of my book, started a ministry program with the local college through our church. The church is growing, there are new ministries working at, and through our local church.

Work was still very busy. I was still working overtime. All of us working together in that small area were getting along well together. I had told the other two co-workers, Bridget and Joyce, who had been moved into our work area, about the book I was writing and asked if they wanted to read some of it. They both said yes so I gave them a few pages to read. A few days later they gave them back. They said they enjoyed reading it and were surprised at some of the hardships I had been through. Joyce said to me that if I could go through what I had gone through in my life and had turned out to be the person I was now that she knew at work, then there was hope for everyone.

Yes, indeed, there is hope for everyone. And the greatest hope of all is the hope we put in knowing Jesus as our Lord and Savior. Amen.

After that point in time, at work it just seemed like all five of us in my work area were beginning to bond together. Not just like regular co-workers who just kind of deal with each other the best we can until the work day is over, but actually caring for one another. Asking about one's friends or families and really caring about the answers that are given. Sympathizing for each other when we are in pain or hurting for whatever reason it might be. Whether it be a headache, backache, or emotional problems. I really felt like we had become more like a family and not just co-workers.

When I showed up at work one Monday morning not at all in my chipper self, my co-workers noticed I was very quiet, not one of my normal traits. One by one they began to ask me what was the matter was something wrong? As I began to share with them what was bothering me that morning, I knew they cared. Our first dog we had gotten some twelve years earlier had died during the night before.

Our male dog, Buddy, was a german shepherd and lab mixed. We had gotten him from another co-worker. And because we did not want him to be lonely, we also got a female, Holly, a husky collie mixed dog. Hence the names Buddy, Holly. Those two pups brought a lot of fun to our home. The kids loved the pups and played with those pups. We have pictures of them running in the snow their first winter. Trying to climb the door steps outside when they were pups. And one of my favorite pictures of Buddy was of him eating crumbs out of a chicken bucket, lying on the floor. Three-quarters of Buddy's body was in the bucket that's how small he was as a pup. But he had become old and hadn't been well for a couple of months. I knew his death was coming but did not want to have to deal with it at that time. Beva, Mom, had only gone to be with the Lord a month earlier and we were still doing our best to cope with that loss in our lives.

I had talked with Hook about it at work and we prayed together that God might take Buddy from us, so that I would not have to put him to sleep. He had put his dog to sleep and I did not want to have to do that too. The night Buddy died I laid in bed thinking he was not going to make it through the night. That I should go downstairs where he was laying and be with him. But I didn't, I said my prayers and went to sleep. Diana woke me in the morning and told me Buddy had died during the night. It was an answered prayer but not one I liked.

Then the next few days I felt terrible because I did not go downstairs and stay with our dog. I wasn't sure he was going to die. I just had a feeling he was. But that morning at work when I shared with my co-workers why I was quite and sad, I not only began to cry but they began to cry with me. They felt my pain, they shared my sorrow, and they did their best to comfort me. That's family. The next few days were not easy but God help me through them.

Once again I relied on Philippians 4:13 (KJV) *I can do all things through Christ which strengtheneth me.* I can make it through each day that I live and breathe here on this earth no matter what that day might bring. Whether it be good things or bad things to deal with, God is my strength.

One of my co-workers, Nina, got a report that one of her sons was having chest pains and had gone to the hospital. She told us about her son going to the hospital but kept on working. Two of our co-workers talked to her and she decided to leave work and go to the hospital. She was in such shock from the news of her son that she was just standing there working and not talking. But the other two co-workers convinced her to go. They could tell she wanted to go but was trying to keep her mind off of her son's situation by working.

The next day she came back to work and ask me to pray for him. I prayed not only for him but for Nina also. She was working ten hour days and then traveling to the hospital after work to see him. He eventually got a defibulator put underneath his skin to keep his heart beating regularly. When we pray for someone it shows them that we really do care for them. You can act like you care, you can say you care, but when you pray for them or their loved ones you prove that you really do care. Want to prove to God how much you care for him? You thank him for your food, your daily bread he provides for you each day, pray to him and thank him for it. God loves when we give him thanks for our daily bread, physical and spiritual food. Want to prove to someone you really do care? Pray for them, then they will know you care.

About three weeks after Buddy died, another one of our dogs died. Daisy Mae, a female purebred beagle we had gotten from another co-worker who had moved away. She was an outside dog whereas Buddy and Holly were inside dogs. Daisy Mae was about thirteen years old. She had not seemed to be sick so her death was a shock. I came home from work and found her laying out side her dog house dead. So I buried her under the apple trees out back next to Buddy. When Diana got home, I had to tell her and we both cried together. Now we had lost Mom and two of our dogs in two months. I went to work and told my co-workers about Daisy Mae and they again did their best to comfort me. I just did my best to dig deeper and deeper in God's word to give me strength to deal with my trials that seemed to hit me all at once.

In September Diana and I got away for the weekend for some camping. We had not camped since Mom had died. We were busy helping take care of Joe. The reservations had already been paid and we needed a break. Our church was going to be having church services, baptism, and a picnic dinner at the lake that weekend. We got to camp with Pastor Dave and his family for the first time that year. We took out the sailboat and talked for a while. Brian and his family were camping that weekend also, along with Robb and Barbara and their daughter Hanna who we had camped with earlier that summer. Doug, our new executive minister, his wife and five children were camping too. Then there were some folks coming and spending one night with campers already there. Hook and Anna finally were going to stay the night at the campground with Brian and his family in their fifth-wheel camper.

Saturday was a beautiful day. We walked, we talked, and we just hung out with each other. Saturday night there were about thirty to thirty-five people showed up at camp and we sat around the camp fire and listened and sang songs. We had praise and worship service at the camp site that night. We were having so much fun the time just flew by. Before we knew it the park rangers stopped by to tell us it was 10:00 pm. Quiet time had arrived.

The next day we were to have church services and then the picnic. Our son Nicholas had built a big spit cooker for Pastor Dave and had brought it to camp. I was going to help a couple of other guys watch the chickens cook during the church services, which were being held right across from our campsite. But Sunday morning came and Diana had gotten a bad migraine headache during the night, so I had to take her to the hospital. The morning at the hospital went quicker than usual so we were back to camp before the church service was over. We were able to see the baptism part of the service. It had begun to rain slightly, but that did not stop us. We had our picnic and then everyone helped each other pack up for home. The end was not what we had hoped for but the weekend was definitely what Diana and I needed, except for her headache.

In October we had another fence to climb, another barrier to overcome. Our youngest son was to be married. He was going to be married on my birthday, which had also been Beva's birthday. Levi lives five hours away on the other side of the state. We had made plans to go to the wedding and had hotel reservations already made. Diana was feeling some reservations about going to the wedding because her mother Beva had been looking forward to going. Plus we didn't want Joe left by himself to think about Beva on her birthday. So naturally this made Diana and me both sad and concerned. But when the time came for us to go to the wedding, other family members were going to spend time with Joe and make sure he got to church on Sunday.

The wedding was on Saturday at 2:00 in the afternoon. We were going to get up around 4:30 that morning and head out on our trip by 5:00. It was a five hour drive. Then we'd stop at our hotel room get cleaned up and head for the wedding. We would attend the wedding and the reception, then go back to our hotel. We'd sleep in the next morning, Sunday, and then head back home.

Diana and I prayed before we left the house, stopped and had breakfast in town, and then started on our five hour trip. I brought along my Bible CDs to listen to while driving. For the first couple of hours, Diana nodded in and out of sleep mode. Eventually she awoke listened to the CDs and we would talk.

We held up pretty good on our trip until we made it to our destination. We got checked into our room and then Diana broke down. She began to cry. I tried to console her, but I also began to cry myself. After a while we just prayed together for God to help us through this special time in our lives. Our youngest son was getting married and we were there to celebrate it with him and his bride.

The wedding was beautiful, the food was good, and all our children were there to celebrate it with them. My ex-wife and her family were there as well. I had the opportunity to visit with her and her family whom I had not seen for many years. We spent time with our grandchildren and Courtney and Levi had a special surprise for me. The DJ had everyone come hold hands and walk around the bride and groom while a song was playing. The DJ called it the circle of family and friends. When the song finished, before we sat down the DJ announced, "Where is Kermit?" I raised my hand and he pulled me into the circle with the bride and groom. They presented me with a beautiful chocolate cake and they all sang happy birthday to me. Now that was a special moment for me, but I could not help but think how great it would have been if Beva had been there to share this moment with me. I hugged my son and his new bride and then hugged Diana, for I knew what she was thinking as tears ran down her face.

We stayed until the reception was over and went to our hotel room. As we sat there talking about the day's events we decided to get up early and try to make it to church on time, even though we were five hours away. Diana set the clock for 4:30 in the morning. We got up, loaded up the car, stopped for breakfast and headed for home. We listened to the Bible CDs on the ride home also. Before I knew it we were home. We ran in the house, cleaned up real fast, and made it to church by 10:40. Our second church services started at 10:45.

We walked up to where our family was sitting. Joe looked up and said, "What are you doing here?"

We just laughed and said, "Coming to church. What are you doing here?"

Diana and I just did not want to miss church. We wanted to be in fellowship with other believers. We wanted to praise and worship God with our family. We needed the fellowship of other believers to continue to help us through this difficult time in our lives. Sometimes even though God lives in us, if we are a Christian, we feel more comforted when we are in the church building on Sunday morning with other believers. Hebrews 10:25 says, "Let us not give up meeting together, as some are in the habit of doing, but let us encourage one another."

Joyce, one of my co-workers began sharing with me about a family she was trying to help through a tough time. She was talking and helping a young woman that had four children and was pregnant with another child. Her husband had left her and she was having a hard time dealing with everything she was going through. Joyce told me that after reading part of my book that it made her look at life differently. She just felt like she was to help this woman and her children, so she has been talking to her on the phone and helping out when needed. The young woman had her new baby a few weeks later and Joyce and her daughters, Kaylee and Kara, have been going over and helping the young woman out by watching her children on occasions. And also to help teach the children of this young woman, to try and help out their mother any way they can. Joyce and her daughters have given up some of their own desires to help someone else during a time of need. Philippians 2:3-4, "Do nothing out of selfish ambition or vain conceit, but in humility consider others better than yourselves, Each of you should look not only to your own interests, but also to the interests of others."

Fast forward a couple of months into December. Joyce, along with some other co-workers, got the whole factory involved with making sure that young woman and her children had a nice Christmas. These co-workers got our management involved also. They collected money from the factory employees, and the company management matched whatever they collected. They did a 50-50 raffle. They put up a paper for individuals to buy presents for the family. Also at least two of our co-workers that I know about (J.R. and Bill) went to that family's house and put up dry wall in the baby's room that had been started but needed finished.

Now the company I work for is a very charitable company. They help different organizations all the time. But I never in my twenty-three years of working there saw so many people get involved in helping out one family or one cause as they did this family at

Christmas. And it all started with one person helping out another person in her time of need.

The week before Thanksgiving another one of my co-workers, Bridget, was going to Florida during the Thanksgiving holidays not only for Thanksgiving but also to celebrate her grandmother's ninetieth birthday. The day before she was to leave she told me she was only going to work eight hours the next day instead of ten hours. She was going to be leaving two hours earlier than everyone else to make it to the airport on time for her flight. The next day, from the time I woke up I felt the Holy Spirit wanting me to pray with her before she left for her trip. Bridget is one of my co-workers who has been reading parts of my book as I write it. She is a person who has listened as I have shared things about not only my life but about God, and she also has talked to me about God and church also. But I was not sure about asking her if I could pray for her at work with other co-workers around. I did not know how she would react. I was afraid she might tell me no and then I wasn't sure how I would react to that. So all day long I kept thinking I need to ask her if I can pray for her. And I just worried that she would not want me to, so I just kept putting it off.

Finally she put on her coat and was telling our other co-workers around us goodbye. They were telling her to have a nice trip and see you after Thanksgiving. When she came by my work area I finally just said, "May I pray for you before you leave on your vacation?"

She looked at me and said, "Yes, will you?"

Oh, what a relief off of my mind. I asked, she said yes, and then I prayed. Wasn't a fancy prayer, just a prayer for her to have a good time away from work, a good time spent with her family and friends in Florida and for God to protect her on her trip there and back. She said thanks and left. I felt better because I had done what God wanted me to do.

After praying for her one of my other co-workers who was close enough to hear me pray for her said that she was nervous about going on this trip even though she has gone to Florida many times before. I was so glad I obeyed what the Holy Spirit was nudging me to do after hearing that. I told Nina and Joyce I would pray for them or anyone they knew anytime they wanted me to. They said, "Yes we know." I had already prayed for and with Nina before. But Joyce said okay and two minutes later gave me the names of a couple of people she wanted me to pray for.

The Monday after Thanksgiving Bridget came back to work. We were still working ten hours a day so we had to be there at 5:00 a.m. We were all glad to see she made it back okay. As we asked about her trip she began to tell us that she had just gotten home in time to make it to work. She did not get to go to bed the night before at all. She was supposed to be back home from Florida by 10:00 p.m. the night before, but the first two planes she was to leave on had mechanical problems and by the time they had a third plane ready the weather was bad and they had to delay her flight. So we were very happy to have her back safe and sound. She worked four hours and then went home for some needed rest.

About two weeks later Bridget came over to my work area and told me doctors had taken a biopsy from her throat the day before. They were checking to see if it might be cancerous. As she finished telling me this she asked, "Would you pray for me?"

I said, "Yes, I will." After praying I talk to her for a few minutes and told her try not to worry, that I had gone through a similar thing and that my mind almost had me convinced that I had cancer just like my mother had and that I was going to die. But that I changed my attitude and trusted in the Lord. I told her to just relax and everything would be okay. If the results came back and they were cancerous, then we would deal with that situation then. But for now, just trust in the Lord that there is no cancer whatsoever. Think positive thoughts.

I continued to pray for her and had asked some brothers and sisters at church to pray for her also. About two weeks later the results came back: negative for cancer. Thank you Jesus. 1 Thessalonians 5:16-18, "Be joyful always; pray continually, give thanks in all circumstances, for this is God's will for you in Christ Jesus."

We need to always pray to the Lord in every circumstance, we may not know what the outcome may be but we can rely on this. God is in control, and if we would just trust in him he will see us through everything that comes our way.

Chapter Eleven

*B*uddy and Holly were the first dogs we had gotten. Around that same time I had been going rabbit hunting with some of my co-workers and decided to buy myself a beagle for hunting. But it was winter and we did not want the pup outside for the winter by himself, so into the house with Buddy and Holly he came. Then, when the time came for me to train him to hunt, he did not really want to go outside. He would go out for a while and then head for the house. He was spoiled. The dogs were outside during the day in a big dog kennel we had purchased but in the evening they would come inside. Next thing we knew Holly the female husky-collie was starting to get fat. She eventually had two pups pure bred beagle, and husky-collie mixed. We had Buddy, our german shepherd-lab mixed fixed but not, Bo Bob, our pure bred beagle because I thought I would buy a pure bred female some day and have them mate for pups. So here we had these two pups we could not part with. We named them Bonnie and Clyde.

They had just turned ten years old in November when we noticed that Bonnie had somehow gotten a cold, it seemed. But after about three days she began not wanting to eat, but drinking a lot of water. But shortly after she would drink the water she would throw it up. Saturday I did not have to work but Diana did. We had decided the night before that we needed to take her to the Vet. Saturday morning came, Diana went to work and Bonnie just kind of laid around. I would look for her and she would either be upstairs in the clothes basket in the bathroom or in the basement in her and Clyde's kennel. All of a sudden I just began to feel in my spirit that Bonnie was going to die that day, she was not going to make it another day. Diana called me from work and told me the Vet said he could see Bonnie right away. I put a blanket in the floor of my truck, put on her leash and off we went.

As we got into the truck she began to look around, she was happy to be going for a ride. But when we got to the Vet she just sat in my lap and did not move. After a while it was Bonnie's turn to see the Vet. I told him what she was and was not doing. He checked her over and told me Bonnie was very sick. As far as he could tell she was having kidney problems. He took blood and said he would call me within an hour and let me know what he found out.

The ride back was like before. She was walking on the seat and looking out the window of the truck. When we got home she just laid around like before. I still had that same feeling though. The Vet called and confirmed what he had expected her kidneys were failing and she also had diabetes. On Monday morning I was to take her in and the Vet was going to show my wife and me how to give her two shots a day. I told the Vet we were supposed to go to Erie Monday morning because Diana's brother was going to have a heart catheterization done. He told me someone was going to have to bring Bonnie in so he could give her an iv on Monday and kept a watch on her during the day. I told him okay we would work something out. Diana called before she left work to check on Bonnie. I just told her she was at home and that was all. I did not want to tell her over the phone what the Vet said.

After Diana got home I told her and she was sad. Of course, I did not tell her what I felt in my spirit. We went to a local restaurant for some afternoon brunch and then back home. When I got back home I decided I was going to hold Bonnie for a while. While holding her I just prayed to God to give me strength and to be with Diana also. I asked Diana to put in *The Ten Commandments* movie and I would watch that while I held Bonnie. Three and a half hours into the movie Bonnie began to breathe heavy and fast; she would stop for a short while and then repeat it. Diana noticed she was breathing heavy and came over to check on her. Bonnie once again began to breathe hard and fast, and then she just stopped breathing altogether. Diana bent over and was blowing in her nose almost yelling, "Breathe, Bonnie, breathe!"

I told her to just leave Bonnie alone she was gone. I held Bonnie for a few more minutes and cried. I got up out of my chair laid Bonnie in it because that was where she would lay when I was not sitting in it. That was her chair too. I went out back to the apple trees and dug her grave next to Buddy and Daisy Mae.

I came back inside Clyde, Bonnie's brother, and Holly, Bonnie's mother, came over, smelled Bonnie and walked away. I took her outside and buried her. I came back into the house and Diana continued crying as I tried to comfort her.

I tried my best to be strong at this point, but Diana saw it as me not caring as much for Bonnie as I did for Clyde. Clyde is my special dog. He's the dog that Diana would tell to go wake up daddy in the mornings and he would run upstairs and lick my face to wake me up. He follows me everywhere in the house. In the living room he sits in my lap. If I get up to go to the kitchen he is right by my side. If I go to the bathroom he follows me, and when I go to bed he goes to bed with me not before. Diana, once in a while, will go to bed before me and the other dogs would go, but not Clyde. Clyde's daddy might go to the kitchen and get a snack and he did not want to miss out on that.

But then, with tears running down her face, Diana looked at me and asked, "Is God going to take my brother too?" Her brother Bob was going to Erie on Monday for a heart catheterization and possible heart surgery preformed, depending on what the doctors found. I told her no, that Bonnie's death did not mean that Bob was going to die too. Diana and I had been through so much these last six months, starting with the passing away of her mother, then trying to work our schedule around helping to take care of her father. The feeding, visiting, doctor appointments, doing the laundry, grocery shopping, bringing him to church. Then losing our first dog Buddy, then Daisy, and now Bonnie.

Because of all these things we had been going through Diana was now questioning what had we done wrong to make God mad at us. I looked at her and told her God was not mad at us for anything. That all we had been through these past few months were not for punishment. The testing of our faith, maybe, but not punishment. I told her to sit down and read the book of Job, but she was too upset to read.

Now we are not perfect, not by a long shot, but we are headed in the right direction God is calling us to. In Philippians 3:12, the apostle Paul says, "Not that I have already obtained all this, or have already been made perfect, but I press on to take hold of that for which Christ Jesus took hold of me."

Sunday morning as we got ready for church Diana was still pretty upset. I was still trying to be as strong as I could for both of us and hold back my emotions. We got to Joe's to pick him up for church. Diana went inside. I sat there and began thinking about Bonnie and the tears just began to flow. I could not help it. Diana and Joe came out and got in the car and we headed for church. I decided to try and talk to Pastor Doug before the church service to have a quick talk with Diana and to let her know God was not punishing us. Upon arriving at church I found Pastor Doug right away and ask if I might talk to him for a minute. He said of course and we went to his office. My intention was to have him speak to Diana to give her some encouragement but as I began to tell him what had happened the day before. I just broke down and began to cry. So he comforted me first, with a hug, with a word and then with prayer. We then went to find Diana. Pastor Doug told her he was sad for her loss, told her God was not mad at her, and then proceeded to ask her to go home and read the book of Job.

Diana looked at Pastor Doug and said, "Have you been talking to Kermit?"

After church we usually take Joe out for lunch and then take him home. Usually we spend some time with him watching TV or just talking. Bob and Lorna, his wife, came back to Joe's after lunch to tell him that Bob was having a heart catheterization done on Monday. Joe is a major worrier so they wanted to wait until the day before the procedure to tell him.

Joe had many questions and Bob and Lorna tried to answer them the best they could. Joe did not want to go to Erie because that was the same hospital where his wife had died. I talked with Pastor Doug. He said he would stop by and check on Joe if Diana and I wanted to go to Erie to support Bob and his family. Before everyone left Joe's, I had everyone hold hands and I prayed for Joe not to worry, prayed for traveling mercies to Erie and back, prayed for the doctors working on Bob and for peace and calmness for Bob during this ordeal. We went home and that evening Diana sat down and read the book of Job and it seemed to help her.

Monday morning we got up early, stopped for a bite to eat and headed for Erie. I put in my Bible CDs while Diana took a nap. Upon arriving at the hospital we went to Bob's room and spent some time with him before they wheeled him off to do the heart catheterization. The procedure only took about thirty minutes, and then the doctor came out to talk to the family. There had been no change since the last heart catheterization he had done four years earlier. So they did not have to do any angioplasty, a stent, or open heart operation. Hallelujah! While Bob was waking up we all went to get a bite to eat. I was so thankful they did not find anything wrong with his heart. Diana could now feel some sort of relief about her brother being okay. We called Joe and let him know that everything went okay and that we would be by to see him later.

We left Erie and headed for home, stopped by Joe's and took him out for dinner. He told us that Pastor Doug and another member of our church, John, came by and brought him lunch and spent some time with him. Thanks to them, Diana and I were able to go to Erie and spend that time with her brother and his family. Without their help we would have felt guilty leaving Joe home by himself worrying.

Our next hurdle to get over was Christmas. On Sunday after church and lunch Joe's children had a birthday party for him. Joe turned eighty-four so we had some cake and ice cream and celebrated. While we were all there, we got out his Christmas tree and put it up and a couple of the women decorated it for him. Just about the time they finished decorating the tree, a group from our church family stopped by to sing Christmas carols. Joe went to the door opened it and they began to sing. They had no idea how much not only Joe but all of us there needed to hear those carols. Thank you so much, First Baptist Church.

They say the first holidays are the worst to go through after losing a loved one. And how true it was becoming. We had made it through Beva's birthday, we had made it through Thanksgiving and now we had to go through Christmas. No one felt like buying gifts, no one wanted to put up the Christmas decorations, no one really wanted to celebrate Christmas. We missed Beva. We wished she was still here with us. But all the wishing in the world was not going to change what had happened. Beva was not here; she is with the Lord. Beva lives on in our hearts and minds but we had to face reality. We must continue on until the Lord calls us home. So we managed through that day celebrating Joe's birthday, decorating the Christmas tree, and hearing Christmas carols sung from the porch.

We did no shopping for gifts that year. With everything going on in our lives we just did not take the time or want to. About three months earlier Diana had bought a new computer, and I had gotten a laptop that was on sale before Christmas also, so we saw no reason to buy anything else. We did make plans to have the family over to Joe's house for Christmas. That way the grandchildren could stop by and visit Joe and get a bite to eat anytime after 1:00 in the afternoon. Joe had decided to give the grandchildren money in a card for Christmas. Diana and I decided we would do the same.

Christmas morning came and Diana was not having a good morning. She said, "It just does not seem like Christmas," and began to cry. I tried to comfort her, but to no avail. We talked about other Christmases and what we had done on them. How her mother and father used to come to our house on Christmas morning when the children were growing up. The more we talked, the worse she got. I fixed us some breakfast and then I went upstairs, took a bath and got cleaned up to go to Joe's house.

When I came back downstairs Diana was still crying. She said, "I'm not going to Dad's." I told her we had made all these plans for the family to go to Joe's house. I had cooked a turkey, other family members were making other foods to eat, and our grandchildren were going over there for Christmas.

Then I told her she could either go upstairs and get cleaned up and ready to go or she could sit in the corner and cry all day. "Which one do you think would make your mother the happiest?" She looked at me with tears in hers eyes and went upstairs and got ready.

We did buy Joe a big fruit basket. When we walked in with it Joe said, "I thought we were only buying for the grandchildren." We told him yes, we did agree to that, but he needed to eat fruit anyway. The family was in and out all afternoon. Family talked, children played, and with God's help we made it through Christmas Day.

New Years Eve Diana and I were invited over to Pastor Dave's house for a cookout. I told Pastor Dave that was our day to feed Joe, so he said to bring Joe along. I told him I would let him know.

I only had to work half a day New Year's Eve, so when I got home I got some food together and went over and spend some time with Joe in the afternoon while Diana was at work. I told him Pastor Dave had invited us over for a cookout, did he want to go? Joe said, "No thanks it's going to be too cold for me but you and Diana go ahead I'll eat what you brought over for dinner."

I told him the next day, New Year's Day, I was going to make a pork roast and sauerkraut and bring it over. Diana and I would eat New Year's Day dinner with him. He thought that was just great. I went home and made a casserole dish of jambalaya for the cookout. Pastor Dave said he was cooking chicken and a beef roast on the spit and someone else was bringing deer and bear so I could bring a side dish or a desert.

We got to Pastor Dave's around 6:30 that evening and already several people were there. Some of them from church we knew but some of them we did not know because they do not come to our church. There were tables set up in his garage with food on them, so I put my jambalaya on one of the tables and went outside. Pastor Dave and a couple of men from our church were taking the beef roast and chickens off the spit and cutting them up. Pastor Dave had a big fire going in his fire pit that reminded me of going camping. As I stood by the fire another man from our church rode up on a four-wheeler who was giving rides to some of Pastor Dave's cookout guests.

We all went inside. Pastor Dave said grace and eating began. There was no shortage of food let me tell ya. There were all kinds of appetizers, chips and dips, cheese and meat trays, fruit pizza. There were the four different kinds of meat, chicken, beef, deer, and bear. And several different side dishes, potatoes, beans, macaroni salad just to name a few. And then the desserts, which were all good, I'm sure, but my favorite (and also a few others) was Brenda, Pastor Dave's wife's, Ho-Ho Cake. It was the best. And of course all the pop or bottled water we could drink. We sat around eating and talking with friends from church just fellowshipping with one another.

After eating a couple of the men from church began giving rides on their four-wheelers on trails through the woods. They were going through mud and a stream that runs through Pastor Dave's property. It started with the children. First they would get all bundled up in their coats and gloves and knit hats and off they would go. A little while latter a couple of more children would get a turn. Then they started taking the adults. I thought to myself *I'm not going on a four-wheeler ride it's too cold.* They were riding through mud and a stream. They would come back and stand in the garage to warm up or by the fire outside to dry their pants off.

But later on Pastor Dave asked me if I wanted to go for a ride in his gator with him. Now for those who don't know what a gator is, a gator is sort of like a four-wheeler except Pastor Dave's gator has six wheels. Gators are use on farms like four-wheelers to do chores around the farm but also for recreation too. Gators also (as an option) have cabs where the riders sit. I thought to myself...*Self, you will be okay riding on the gator. It has a cab and I won't get cold or wet.*

As we left on the ride we began talking as we were plowing through the muddy trails. Pastor Dave asked how Diana and I were doing, about our son Nicholas, how he was, and also about how Joe was holding up through the holidays. As we were talking we were going through places in the woods I never thought that machine would go. We were following one of the four-wheelers and everywhere that four-wheeler went we went also without missing a beat.

Then all of a sudden Pastor Dave went right when the four-wheeler went left. I thought to myself *the four-wheeler must be going through a difficult area so Pastor Dave is taking the easy route.* I should have known better than to even think such a thing because that just isn't Pastor Dave. And guess what, myself was wrong! Pastor Dave took us down a steep hillside and through the stream below with water about two feet deep. As we made the splash into the stream the water rose up high enough to leak into the cab area. My pants got wet clear up to my knee. So much for being inside a cab. If the water is higher than where the cab is connected you are going to get wet. We then climbed a huge bank on the other side and before I knew it we were back to his garage. I got out of the gator stood by the fire to dry my pants and to stay warm.

As the evening went on I would talk to different people that stopped by the fire ring and watched as one by one others took their turns riding on the four-wheelers. About 9:30 we said our thanks to Pastor Dave and Brenda for the invitation and headed home.

New Year's Day I awoke early. As I lay in bed I thought about the past year. Especially the last part of the year and all the trials Diana and I had been through. How God had given us strength when we thought we had none left. When God had given us joy at times when we thought we had none left. Whenever we had put our trust in God and his word he had and continues to see us through every situation that comes our way. When we finally realize in this life that we are nothing without God, that only true joy and true happiness can only come from having a relationship with God, that everything we go through in this life is to draw us to God, when we finally realize that we were born to serve God and not God serving us: that's when we finally realize that true faith, true hope, and true love is all that matters.

I put on the pork roast in the slow cooker for about three hours then added the sauerkraut and cooked for another thirty minutes. Diana and I went over to Joe's where I heated up mashed potatoes to eat with our pork roast and sauerkraut. We sat down, said grace and began eating. While we were eating and talking Joe said to Diana and me, "Thanks for coming over and spending New Year's Day with me. I thought I would be like many other old people that live by themselves. I thought I would be spending New Year's Day alone." We told him we were glad to spend the day with him. We finished eating Diana and Joe did the dishes while I turned on the TV. After they had finished doing the dishes they came out to the living room and took turns taking naps while I watched TV. What a day!

New Year's Day we were fed and spent time with someone who loves us and whom we love. That's all anybody in this life really wants, isn't it? We want to be fed and we want to be loved. Both of those things we can receive here in this life from other people. But that kind of food and that kind of love is only temporal. Real food and real love can only come from God. Real food we can only receive from God by reading or hearing his Word. Real love we can only receive by having a relationship with God. By receiving real food and real love from God then we are able to share what we have with others so that they might have real food and real love also. Although the food and the love I receive from people is good, the food and the love I receive from God is the Greatest of all.

Chapter Twelve

*E*cclesiastes 4:10-12 says, "If one falls down, his friend can help him up. But pity the man who falls and has no one to help him up! Also if two lie down together, they will keep warm. But how can one keep warm alone? Though one may be overpowered, two can defend themselves. A cord of three strands is not quickly broken."

As I have set down my life in written form over the past few months I realized something. That just like the Israelites wandering around in the desert for forty years before entering the promised land, I have spent the better part of my forty years of being a Christian wandering around in my own desert. Just like the Israelites, when things were going the way they liked or planned or by their own desires they were happy and content. But whenever something changed from their thinking, their liking, their desires, or when trouble came their way, they would turn from God and do their own thing. And I have seen the evidence of those same mistakes throughout my life also, until I finally came to the point in my life where I realized that no matter how hard I tried, no matter how hard I wanted to on my own. I could not live up to the expectations my Father in heaven has in store for me to accomplish. I might get a few right, I might even accomplish some great feats on my own, but nothing like we can accomplish with God as our guide.

How do we do that? The same way that I have learned to do it. By surrendering and trusting God totally. What do I mean by surrendering? I mean our whole life and everything that comes with it. Our good times, our bad times. Surrender it all to God. After you have surrendered your life over to God then you need to trust God. Trust not only in God our Father in heaven, trust not only in Jesus his Son, but trust also in the Holy Spirit whom God our Father and Jesus his Son have sent to us to guide our lives.

I believe the reason so many Christians are living unfulfilled or even defeated Christian lives is this: they have not been using the power God the Father and Jesus his Son intended for them to use. The Holy Spirit. A cord of three strands is not quickly broken. The Father, the Son, the Holy Spirit. As Christians we began to hear about God the Father and creator in all kinds of ways. Either from our parents, relatives, neighbors, co-workers, church, television, radio, or books to name a few. Then at some point we realize we need to be saved from our sins, so enters the son of God, Jesus. We ask him into our hearts to save us from our sins. And thus begins our Christian life.

The next thing I believe is very critical in our Christian life and that is being baptized. Jesus speaking in Matthew 28:19, "Therefore go and make disciples of all nations, baptizing them in the name of the Father and of the Son and of the Holy Spirit." Why is that so important? Because Jesus knew that Christians not only needed to accept the Father, the Son and the Holy Spirit. That Christians not only needed to believe in the Father, the Son and the Holy Spirit.

But that Christians also needed to trust in the Father, the Son and the Holy Spirit. Not just one, not just two, but all three. Christians trust that God the Father created us. They trust that Jesus his Son saved us. What do Christians trust the Holy Spirit for? We need to trust the Holy Spirit for power. What kind of power? The kind of power to live our Christian lives in victory.

Think about it. When was the last time you heard a sermon on the Holy Spirit? Not just in the context of the sermon, but the text itself. Christians cannot live the life that God intended for them to live without the power of the Holy Spirit working in their lives. The Holy Spirit does many things in the life of a Christian and I'm not going to cover them all. But two that will benefit us tremendously in our Christian walk are these. The Holy Spirit gives Christians the power to be witnesses of Jesus Christ and the Holy Spirit give Christians the power to do the ministry of Jesus Christ. John 15:26 says, "When the Counselor comes, whom I will send to you from the Father, the Spirit of truth who goes out from the Father, he will testify about me."

The Counselor, the Spirit of Truth, who is the Holy Spirit, when he comes to a Christian he is to testify about Jesus Christ to us and through us. How does the Holy Spirit do that? By empowering us to live the kind of life Jesus did. Jesus is our example to live by. Jesus talking to his disciples in John 15:4-5 (KJV) *Abide in me, and I in you. As the branch cannot bear fruit of itself, except it abide in the vine; no more can ye, accept ye abide in me. I am the vine, ye are the branches: he that abideth in me, and I in him, the same bringeth forth much fruit: for without me ye can do nothing.*

Jesus is the vine Christians are the branches and the Holy Spirit is the sap or power that runs from the vine through the branches to produce fruit. What kind of fruit does Jesus want to produce through Christians? In Galatians 5:22, the Apostle Paul writes,

"But the fruit of the Spirit is love, joy, peace, patience, kindness, goodness, faithfulness, gentleness, and self-control." On our own we might be able to artificially produce some fruits. But we cannot produce all of them on our own. Through the power of the Holy Spirit working in us and through us the Holy Spirit can produce them. Not artificial fruit but pure fruit because it's coming from God not us. It is through the fruit of the Spirit that Christians will be able to become witnesses for Jesus Christ.

Just imagine a Christian witnessing to co-workers telling them how Jesus changed their life. But in reality that Christian seems no different from any other person at work. The Christian shows no love to some of his or her co-workers, only a few close friends. Or the Christian who never seems to have joy or peace, either with themselves or to others. Or maybe the Christian who has no patience or kindness for anyone except for other co-workers that say they are Christians. Or Christians who show no gentleness toward others. And last but not least of all Christians who have no self-control.

The reason Christians have no self-control is because we try and do it ourselves. If Christians would rely on the Holy Spirit instead of ourselves, self-control would simply become control. When we let the Holy Spirit work in our lives and change us little by little into the likeness of Jesus, we become better witnesses. It takes the Holy Spirit to produce fruit in us that will empower us to act or live a life more like Jesus. Then as we live a life that shows fruit consistent with the way Jesus life was, people are more likely to listen to what you have to say about your Christian faith.

Fruit begins with what? A seed. When we become Christians, some things God changes instantly but others take time. The fruit of the Spirit does not come instantaneously. It begins as a seed. The Holy Spirit plants that seed in our hearts and our minds. As we grow in Christ studying the word of God, praying and seeking him first in our lives, that seed will begin to grow and in due season it will produce in and through Christians.

Now let's look at the second thing the Holy Spirit's power will do in the life of a Christian. The Holy Spirit gives Christians the power to do the ministry of Jesus Christ. The Holy Spirit does that through the gifts he gives to Christians. In 1 Corinthians 12:1, Paul writes, "Now about spiritual gifts, brothers, I do not want you to be ignorant." Then in verses 7-11, Paul goes into a more detailed description of the gifts. "Now to each one the manifestation of the Spirit is given for the common good. To one there is given through the Spirit the message of wisdom, to another the message of knowledge, by means of the same Spirit, to another faith by the same Spirit, to another gifts of healing by that one Spirit, to another miraculous powers, to another prophecy; to another distinguishing between spirits, to another speaking in different kinds of tongues, and to still another the interpretation of tongues. All these are the work of one and the same Spirit, and he gives them to each one, just as he determines."

As you can see from this last verse it is the Holy Spirit who gives the Christian his or her spiritual gifts. What are we to do with those spiritual gifts? Use them to minister to others. The gifts are given to Christians for service to God toward others. Who are these others I'm talking about? Anyone Christians come in contact with, those others. The Christian who knows his or her gifts, will benefit from their gifts but those gifts are not given to them alone. Christians are to use their gifts for the same reason Jesus used his spiritual gifts: for the building up of the Kingdom of God.

In Ephesians 4:11-12, Paul writes, "It was he who gave some to be apostles, some to be prophets, some to be evangelists, and some to be pastors and teachers, to prepare God's people for works of service, so that the body of Christ may be built up." These leaders that God has put in charge of the body of Christ were and are being given gifts to help equip Christians to do the same. What's the difference between the leaders and the lay people? The Holy Spirit gifts Christians (lay people) for service mainly outside the four walls of our local church for the Kingdom of God. The Holy Spirit gifts (leaders) for service inside the four walls of the local church. Generally speaking, of course though, these acts of service are interchangeable.

Now in 1 Corinthians 12:8-10, we have these nine spiritual gifts. "Message of wisdom, message of knowledge, faith, healing, miraculous powers, prophecy, distinguishing between spirits, speaking in different kinds of tongues, and interpretation of tongues." In the same book of the Bible, same chapter, verse 28 Paul, writing about the body of Christ (Christians), he gives this list of spiritual gifts: "Apostles, prophets, teachers, workers of miracles, healing, helpers, administration, and tongues." In Romans 12:6-8, this is the list of spiritual gifts given: "Prophesying, serving, teaching, encouraging, contributing, leadership, mercy." These are the spiritual gifts list we have from the New Testament.

You might say is that it? Is that all of the spiritual gifts there are? No I'm not saying that, but I believe that all spiritual gifts that Christians do have can be linked back to one of these listed in the New Testament.

You may ask how do I know which spiritual gift or gifts do I have? Ask the Holy Spirit to reveal to you which spiritual gift or gifts you have. Ask the Holy Spirit to guide you in the right direction to discover your gift or gifts. Try out different spiritual gifts to see if you are good at them or not. See which gifts you feel comfortable doing. Those are just a few ways to find out what your gift or gifts might be.

Why are spiritual gifts so important for Christians to use? So that we can do the ministry of Jesus Christ. In Luke chapter 4, Jesus returning from the desert in the power of the Spirit, went into the synagogue and read from the scroll of Isaiah. Verses 18-19, "The Spirit of the Lord is on me, because he has anointed me to preach good news to the poor. He has sent me to proclaim freedom for the prisoners and recovery of sight for the blind, to release the oppressed, to proclaim the year of the Lord's favor."

The first thing we see from these verses is that Christians have to have the power of the Holy Spirit in our lives to do the ministry of Jesus. If Christians are being lead by the Holy Spirit in their daily lives, if the fruit of the Spirit is present in the Christians life, then the power of the Holy Spirit is there. Then Christians are to preach the good news to the poor.

"Preach the good news?" you might say. "I could never do that."

Simply put it just means Christians are to tell non-Christians what Jesus did for us and them by dying on the cross of Calvary and rising from the dead.

Christians are to proclaim freedom for the prisoners. Who are the prisoners? Again the non-Christians are. They are trapped in a prison of sin and death. Christians are to show them how to live a victorious life in Jesus where sin and death does not enslave us any longer.

Christians are to help recover sight to the blind. How are Christians to do that? When Christians tell non-Christians the good news and they believe. The Bible says their spiritual eyes will be opened. Non-Christians have a covering over their eyes that blinds them to the truth, until they believe the good news, and then the Bible says the covering is removed and they can now see.

Christians are to help the oppressed. How are we to do that? By Christians telling and showing by example to non-Christians that nothing in this world or the spiritual world can keep us down as long as Jesus Christ is the Lord of our life. That our rest is in God alone.

And finally as Christians we need to proclaim to non-Christians the favor of the Lord in our lives. How are we to do that? Share with non-Christians favors or blessings, big or small, the Lord has brought into our lives. The most important one of all being this: that a Christian is a member of the family of God. That a Christian has a relationship with God. That a Christian can know God in a personal way. That God loves us, cares for us, and will guide us through the power of the Holy Spirit to live our lives for him. That the creator of the universe, the creator of life itself, God has now become our Father.

From using just this one example from the scriptures we can see how the Holy Spirit will use Christians to do the ministry of our Lord Jesus Christ. The gifts of the Spirit are given to all Christians for the ministry work of Jesus Christ. Galatians 5:25 (KJV) *If we live in the Spirit, let us also walk in the Spirit.* How is that possible? By faith. The Bible says in Hebrews 11:6, "And without faith it is impossible to please God."

How do we get our faith? In Romans 10:17 (KJV*) So then faith cometh by hearing, and hearing by the word of God.* People need to hear the Word of God from Christians. People need to hear the Word of God from pastors and teachers. People need to hear the Word of God from evangelists. People need to hear the Word of God from newspapers, books, Christian TV programming, computers, iPods, every possible avenue the Word of God can be seen, heard, or read.

But the most important way to hear the Word of God is from where else? From God himself. Make time everyday to pray to God and to read his Word, the Holy Bible. 2 Timothy 3:16 says, "All Scripture is God-breathed and is useful for teaching, rebuking, correcting and training in righteousness."

As we pray and read the Holy Bible everyday in James 4:8 it says, "Come near to God and he will come near to you." As you come near to God through the power of the Holy Spirit he will guide you in your walk with God. As you listen to the Holy Spirit and he guides you through your life, you cannot help but share your testimony in Jesus Christ with others.

And as you grow in the Lord making Jesus your example in this life here on earth, remember these words from 1 Peter 3:15, "But in your hearts set apart Christ as Lord. Always be prepared to give an answer to everyone who asks you to give the reason for the hope that you have. But do this with gentleness and respect."